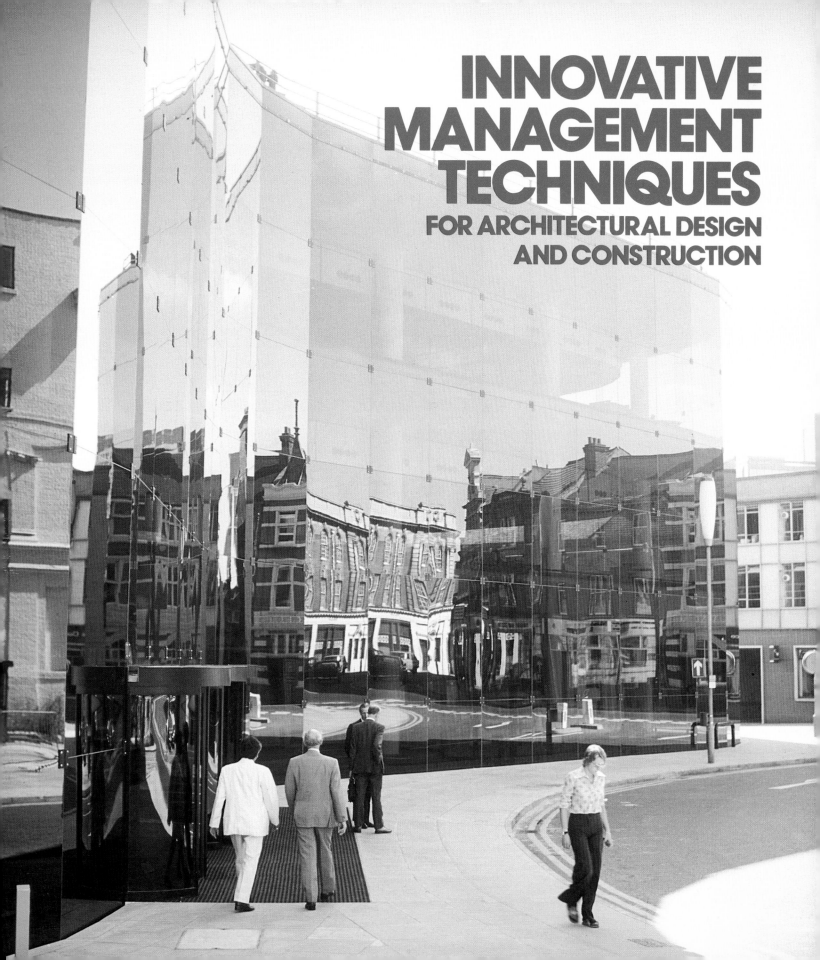

INNOVATIVE MANAGEMENT TECHNIQUES

FOR ARCHITECTURAL DESIGN AND CONSTRUCTION

Overleaf: A blue sky on the reflective glass of the Willis Farber & Dumas offices deemphasizes the bulk of the building designed by Foster Associates in Ipswich, England. The project is shown on pages 128–132.

Right: Color is used to emphasize the depth of the facade in this condominium project in Santa Monica, California, designed by David M. Cooper of A Design Group. The project is shown on pages 173–175.

Below: Designed by Foster Associates to be adjustable, the Sainsbury Center for the Visual Arts at the University of East Anglia in Norwich, England, accommodates a wide range of activities from instruction to exhibition within its flexible area. The project is shown on pages 123–127.

Color and natural daylighting are important design elements in the Hollywood houses designed by Helmut C. Schulitz in Los Angeles, California. The project is shown on pages 169–171.

Left: The amount of slope on the roof of the Nancy Barrett house in Damariscotta, Maine, was not actually determined until the house was framed. Designed by Sellers & Company, the project is shown on pages 114–115.

Above: The vibrant colors of the Talbot house designed by Taft Architects in Nevis, West Indies, reflect vernacular customs. The project is shown on pages 6 (bottom) and 159–160.

Taft Architects paid special attention to harmonize the scale and color of new architectural details with the character of the original Springer Building in Galveston, Texas. The project is shown on pages 164–165.

The center pavilion of the Talbot house designed by Taft Architects in Nevis, West Indies, is open on all sides to catch breezes. Note how stenciling is incorporated into the design here, in contrast with its use in the Springer Building above. The project is shown on pages 159–160.

Opposite page: All the woodwork in the Lucy Mackall house in Cambridge, Massachusetts, was designed by her brother Louis and fabricated in his shop, Breakfast Woodworks. The project is shown on pages 105–107.

Opposite page: The abstract geometric composition of this house in Eagle River, Wisconsin, designed by Murphy/Jahn contrasts with the natural landscape. The project is shown on pages 117–121.

Left: The window pattern of the Minton house in Copake, New York, designed by Alfredo De Vido Associates, Architects, is revealed in this photograph taken at dusk. The project is shown on pages 74–76.

Below: Stock windows are arranged geometrically in Alfredo De Vido's Spechouse 6 in East Hampton, New York, to achieve a striking pattern. The project is shown on pages 77–81.

Above: Aeronautical imagery is combined with solar features in this house in Colorado City, Colorado, designed by Jersey Devil Design/ Construction. The project is shown on pages 102–103.

Right: The building on Columbia Heights in Brooklyn, New York, designed by Alfredo De Vido Associates, Architects, recalls the row of 19th-century Renaissance Revival buildings in its scale and detail. The project is shown on pages 88–91.

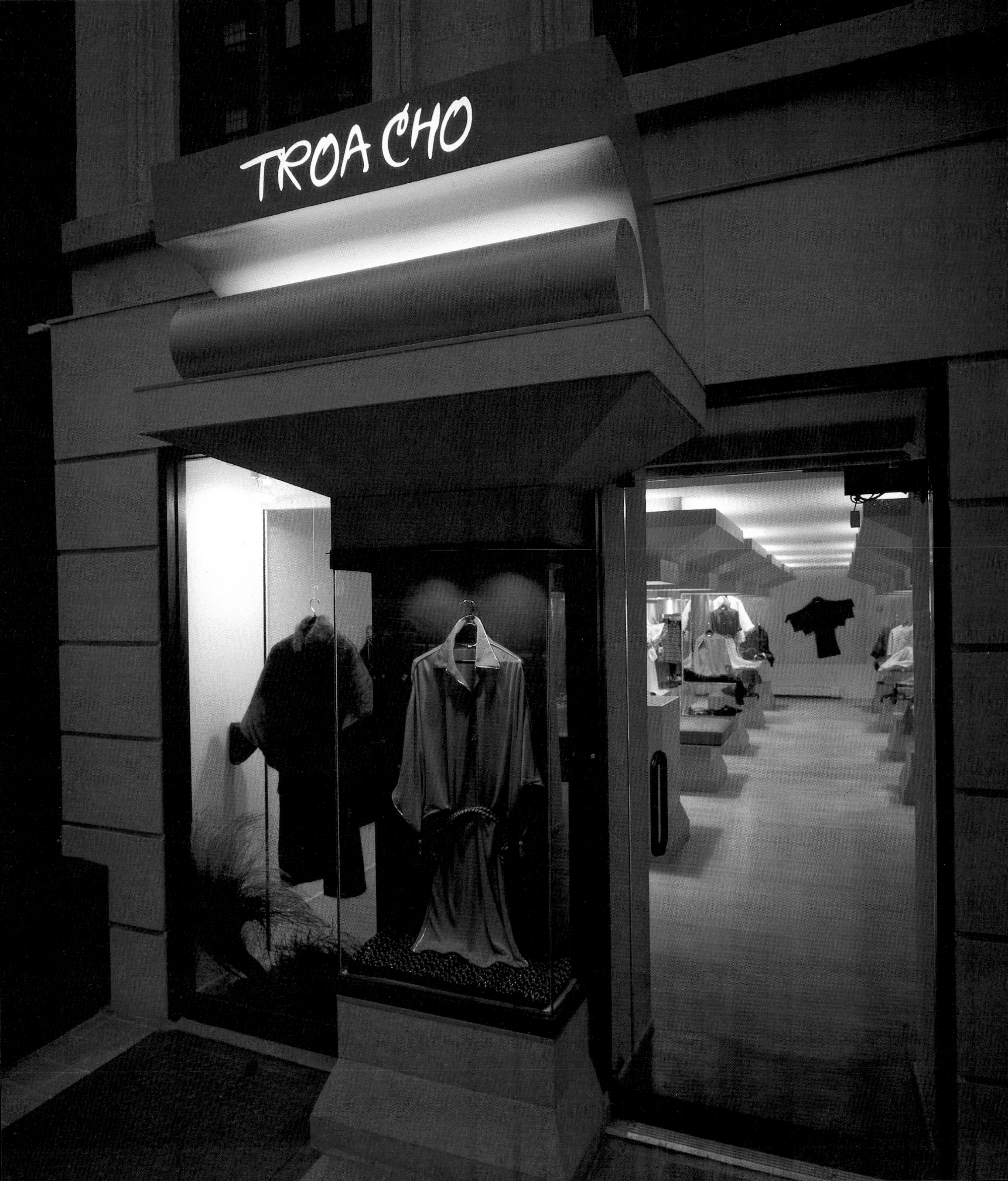
TROA CHO

Left: The logo for Troa Cho, a New York boutique designed by Alfredo De Vido Associates, Architects, was located on top of the display column in keeping with the Landmarks Commission's desire to retain the central pier. The project is shown on pages 67–68.

Above: The bar has a small ladder recalling the name of the restaurant, Die Leiter, and illuminated glass block to provide a striking view while sitting at the bar. Located in Frankfurt, West Germany, it was designed by Jean-Pierre Heim of Design Connection International. The project is shown on pages 51–53.

Above: Tilework surrounds and accents the main entrances of the Masterson Branch YWCA and Metropolitan Administration Building in Houston, Texas, designed by Taft Architects. The project is shown on pages 161–163.

Right: Night lighting for the Village Square shopping center in Houston, Texas, was provided for the entire facade. This renovation was designed by William T. Cannady & Associates, Inc., Architects. The project is shown on pages 195–197.

Above: The low-ceilinged part of the studio in Shigeo Fukuda's house in Tokyo, Japan, is closed off from the high-pitched area in the winter, since that portion of the space is not heated. Designed by Koji Yago, the project is shown on pages 185–187.

Overleaf: The pointed top of Il Teatro del Mondo designed by Aldo Rossi recalls the tower of Piazza San Marco behind it. The project is shown on pages 146–147.

16

INNOVATIVE MANAGEMENT TECHNIQUES

FOR ARCHITECTURAL DESIGN AND CONSTRUCTION

by Alfredo De Vido, FAIA

WHITNEY LIBRARY OF DESIGN
an imprint of Watson-Guptill Publications/New York

To the memory of John Knox Shear, architect and educator, Dean of the Department of Architecture at Carnegie Institute of Technology during my undergraduate years there. His leadership and guidance were greatly admired and appreciated.

Copyright © 1984 by Whitney Library of Design

First Published 1984 in New York by the Whitney Library of Design
an imprint of Watson-Guptill Publications,
a division of Billboard Publications, Inc.,
1515 Broadway, New York, N.Y. 10036

Library of Congress Cataloging in Publication Data
De Vido, Alfredo, 1932
  Innovative management techniques for architectural design and
construction
  1. Architectural design—Case studies. 2. Architecture,
Modern—20th century—Addresses, essays, lectures.
I. Title.
NA2750.D348 1984   721'.068   84-13203
ISBN 0-8230-7291-6

Distributed in the United Kingdom by Phaidon Press Ltd.,
Littlegate House, St. Ebbe's St., Oxford

Manufactured in U.S.A.

First Printing, 1984

1 2 3 4 5 6 7 8 9 / 89 88 87 86 85 84

ACKNOWLEDGMENTS

I would like to extend thanks to the architects, owners, and builders whose collaborative efforts are described in this book and to the photographers who recorded those efforts so well. Thanks to Stephen A. Kliment, FAIA, and Susan Davis, editors of the Whitney Library of Design, who furnished steady help and encouragement during the development of the book, and to Jay Anning, designer, who accommodated my requests concerning the graphic layouts. Thanks also to my wife and co-worker, Catherine, who assisted in many stages of this project.

CONTENTS

FOREWORD

Every year the task of producing quality architecture becomes more difficult. Our design professions are facing a major challenge to our common goal of the highest design quality within the constraints of budget and schedule. Almost every trend in the construction industry is making the achievement of this goal more complex. Only those firms that are not only creative in design, but also creative in managing the design and construction process, are overcoming these problems and achieving consistent quality in their work. Among the many pressures and trends contributing to this growing complexity are the following:

1. There has been a steady move away from the traditional design/bid/build process to expedited processing, including fast track, construction management, and design/build. These and many other techniques usually call for construction to begin before the completion of the design process. This places great time pressure on architects to anticipate, define, and coordinate those building elements most important to the project's design and technical quality.

2. Coincident with the increase in the use of the term "construction management" has been an apparent decline in the number of qualified managers and senior "craftsmen" in the construction industry. This decline not only makes quality control more elusive but also has made cost and schedule management more difficult for all members of the project team.

3. Clients have become increasingly sophisticated, involved, and demanding. Growing client involvement in the hundreds of architectural decisions where design intent and goals are balanced against cost, function, and other criteria often limits the architect's freedom to direct and control the achievement of project excellence.

4. Open and developable sites are gone in most areas; more and more projects require careful and creative responses to an existing structure and site context.

5. There is so much to know to successfully solve the new series of problems presented to most architects. This is true in every aspect of building including: concerns such as energy, environmental protection, or landmark laws; large participation in the design process by specialist consultants or the rapidly growing number of public review agencies; new or rediscovered materials such as the ones used in this era of greater design freedom; and new techniques such as uses of computer-assisted documentation.

6. And in spite of all these factors, fees have become tighter and the profession more competitive, making it even more important for architects to provide their services as efficiently as possible. Nowhere are these pressures more acutely felt than on smaller projects where the fees available do not support a team of specialists to deal with even the normal complexities of any building project. Often one or two people have to make the thousands of decisions involved. Therefore, in order to achieve consistent quality, the architect must continually demonstrate a creativity both in his or her conceptual approach and in structuring and managing the process that develops the concept into a successfully completed project.

In this book, Alfredo De Vido has tackled the ambitious task of researching and illustrating the growing variety of techniques used by architects—in both the United States and overseas—to imaginatively respond to the need for change in the process of designing and building good architecture. No book is, of course, a complete compendium of such techniques. This book serves instead as an introduction that should encourage other architects, builders, and owners to seek their own unique approaches to their projects. The examples in this book are drawn from a variety of leading architects' works. As these case studies prove, quality architecture can result—and often depends upon—a marriage of design and management skill.

Bradford Perkins, AIA, AICP

INTRODUCTION

The intent of this book is to document methods to control the quality of building projects more fully during the entire process. Shown are ways of combining the special skills of architects, builders, and owners to realize design intents on schedule and within budget.

Architects who extend their scope of professional services gain additional satisfaction and remuneration for professional service and in the process also improve their skills. Builders can contribute cost- and time-effective suggestions to the team once they understand that all aspects and phases of construction are complementary. Owners who participate with the architect and the builder in the early stages of a project can supply valuable advice toward their programming, thereby enabling them to fit the design to their needs.

THERE ARE PROBLEMS WITH TRADITIONAL APPROACHES

Other than for large complex buildings with unusual site or program demands, there is little participation either by the architect in the project management of building construction or by builders and owners in the design process. Architects at present restrict their role to observing construction and concentrate on the design phases of the building. Project management for large buildings is handled by a corps of professionals who specialize in organizing budgets, schedules, and work-flow from the inception of the project. For smaller projects architects are called in when the program is well defined to do the design and construction documents. These are then turned over to a group of

qualified contractors who bid the work. Upon selection, one of them builds the project, subject to the architect's and owner's approval that the work has been carried out within the design intent and built in a satisfactory and safe manner.

There are some problems with this approach:

· The program furnished to the architect may not fit the owner's intent, budget, or site.

· During the important design period when many decisions are made affecting quality and budget, the builder of the project is not present. Unless the architect is unusually conversant with the pricing and construction techniques, some decisions may be made that will not produce the desired esthetic and economic goals. For example, the architect may specify the application of stucco in an unusual way that cannot be handled by most local builders. The few that can handle the technique will probably reflect this with a higher price.

· The selected builder and his subcontractor may not be the best team to do all the tasks in the project. Even a small building like a house is a very complex object, requiring that skills of many types of craftsmen be scheduled and coordinated.

· The reduction of the architect's role to a designer and producer of paper documents that are realized by others has resulted in a wide-scale bypassing of his or her skills. Owners may decide to go directly to a builder, thinking that the money paid for an architect's services is

not justified functionally or esthetically.

· During construction, the architect may lose control, to the detriment of the project and relations with the owner.

HISTORICAL BACKGROUND

The present system of architectural practice has evolved historically. Professionals who restrict their activities and earn their livelihood solely from the design of buildings are a relatively modern phenomenon.

Egyptian and Greek "architects" spent most of their time on site, organizing and directing stone cutters and sculptors. Romans worked out their engineering feats on site, solving their problems in a practical ad hoc manner. In Gothic, Renaissance, and Baroque times there was an increasing reliance on drawings, and a group of men engaged in the design of buildings emerged. However, this was not their sole activity, since many building designers were sculptors and painters as well.

Due to the fact that the United States was carved out of a hostile wilderness, practical skills have always been prized and possession of them raised to an ideology. In England, which is the source of many of the early attitudes that shaped this country, architects were frequently talented amateurs such as Christopher Wren or masons and carpenters such as Nicholas Hawksmoor. In the 18th-century buildings got more complex, and professionals such as Sir John Soane spent a good part of their time on horseback or in a carriage visiting jobs under construction, giving instruction to the trades, ordering materials, and keeping meticulous cost accounts of these activities. One of Soane's skills much appreciated by his clients was his ability to control costs and schedules.

In the middle of the 19th century there was still insufficient work to keep professionals busy designing only buildings. Victorian architects, for example, arranged leases and rents and managed buildings for their clients. They preferred to spend their time designing, but there was not enough work to keep them going.

Charles Bulfinch in the late 18th and early 19th centuries was one of the first people who earned his living solely through the design of buildings. Most houses, however, were done by carpenters, then called "housewrights," who used plan books to help them in esthetic matters.

In the latter part of the 19th century, architectural schools such as MIT and Columbia made their appearance respectively in 1865 and 1881, and design was institutionalized, with a Beaux-Arts approach emphasizing art as the prime goal of the architect. Practicality and economy were downgraded. Richard Morris Hunt, one of the leading practitioners of the day, regularly exceeded estimates, neglected supervision, and disregarded the client's programs. Despite problems and lawsuits, he was articulate, talented, and able to gain prestigious commissions steadily. However, there were practical architects such as H. H. Richardson and Chicago firms such as Adler and Sullivan or Burnham and Root that dominated the construction of commercial buildings in that city in the late 19th century.

The Beaux-Arts approach fostered the attitude that practicality should be subordinated to esthetics. Clients who were able to supply the money to build buildings based on this philosophy were and remain few.

Since American culture is frequently characterized by commercial and technical bias, many construction decisions are made by real estate developers, estimators, and contractors without benefit of architectural judgment. One of the reasons for this is the popular belief that architects still practice with Beaux-Arts attitudes and are willing to sacrifice owner's budgets and timetables to esthetic goals. Although this attitude is still with us, there are many architects who realize the value of early cooperation with owners and builders and take a serious view of their professional commitments in all areas. This has resulted in new roles for architects such as programmer, builder, entrepreneur, or consultant to other architects.

In the planning stages this book was going to deal solely with small buildings—houses, shops, small offices. However, in talking with architects and looking at their work it became clear that moderate-sized and simple large buildings must be included, because of the many opportunities they provide to use these new approaches. For such projects, especially those built away from large cities, the time is ripe for traditional methods of managing the design and construction to give way to innovation. These types of buildings make up a large majority of what is built today, and that's where the opportunities are.

A COMPENDIUM OF APPROACHES

Conventional procedures for designing and constructing buildings are not always in the owner's best interests, nor do they always produce the best architecture. Based on the projects and their owners, architects, and builders described in this book, this chapter summarizes how innovative procedures can be used or tailored to produce better buildings more efficiently and at lower cost.

DESIGN APPROACHES

Design is that part of the building process where the architect identifies and analyzes the client's requirements (the program) and goes on to prepare drawn and written documents that form the framework for construction of the building. Under conventional methods of practice, this phase is isolated to produce documents from which a contractor computes a sum of money he feels is needed to build the building. However, distinct lines of separation between design and construction are often inappropriate and undesirable. Following are some practical hints on alternate methods and procedures.

PROGRAM THE BUILDING WITH THE OWNERS

Most building programs are well formulated by the time they reach the architect. However, you can make a major impact on the building by questioning the need for and use of proposed spaces in a building. Among the firms represented in this book, Foster, Stirling, and Aldington, Craig and Collinge stress the importance of shaping the program with the owner.

This seems to be a distinctly English practice, in which the architect sees himself as much more than a service professional in the programming phase. These architects believe that their knowledge of the techniques of design and construction can help determine not only space but also psychological needs. They do it because they believe that an architect's training can be a healthy part of the programming. Among the ideas found in the presentation of these firms' work are the following five examples:

Use easy-to-understand graphics to explain the necessity for building. This cartoon was used to gain support in a convincing, appealing way for a projected move out of the city from employees of the Willis Faber & Dumas offices. Foster Associates built the new offices in Ipswich, England.

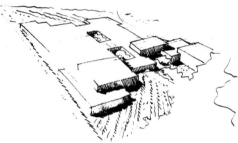

Explain broad building concepts to the owner with simple block sketches. This sketch by Foster Associates showed the client at IBM Technical Park in Greenford, Middlesex, England, that the original idea of flexible space could be expanded outward and upward.

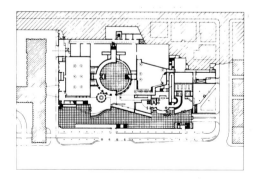

Interpret the program to create a rich sequence of spaces. Although the competition requirements called for an inner court to display sculpture and serve as a circulation device, architects James Stirling & Michael Wilford and Associates freely interpreted this to create a rich central space that became the core of Stuttgart Staatsgalerie in Stuttgart, West Germany.

Turn program problems to advantage by coming up with a unifying design idea. A need to build rapidly in a declining area suggested a grouping of spaces under a quickly erected roof at the North Woolwich Health Center in London, England, designed by Aldington, Craig and Collinge.

Analyze other, similar buildings with the client to help find the best approach for your own project. Examination of other art galleries throughout the world by Foster Associates led to the decision that a common roof for the entire gallery was the right one for this collection at the Sainsbury Center for the Visual Arts in Norwich, England.

WORK WITH THE CLIENTS' PROGRAM AND BUDGET

Working directly with the clients in formulating a program as shown above is not always easy or practical. The next best approach is to probe beyond the bare program as it is given to you. Since the client may have spent considerable time thinking about the building, understanding the thought behind the program will be to your advantage. It will also give useful insights into how the budget was conceived and may help you suggest ways to modify it.

With smaller work, such as houses, receiving a concise written program from the clients is unusual. Ask for it anyway, explaining that it need not be a polished essay. The program for bigger buildings will generally be more complete since they are often generated by a committee or a group. These will often be accompanied by a careful budget based on similar buildings in the area.

Even with a good written program, it is important to do the following:

When confronted with what looks to be too short a time schedule for construction, ask if the work can be phased or whether there should be a design/build arrangement between architect and builder. Since work could proceed only during the summer months, architects Leung, Hemmler, Camayd, P.C., programmed three phases for the work that did not conflict with the ski season at the Elk Mountain Ski Area in Union Dale, Pennsylvania.

Work up a list of questions affecting the client, builder, site, and budget. The architects in the BumpZoid firm distributed a detailed questionnaire to clients Niejelow/Rodin prior to beginning work on this rebuilding.

A checklist of questions will be useful:

CLIENTS

· What rooms are required? Which ones are essential? Which are the most important? Which could be combined? Which could be eliminated if necessary? Is there a summary of total square footage (metrics)?

· What activities will take place in individual spaces?

· What key words describe the client's vision of the building? Snug, cozy? Spacious? Striking? Unpretentious? Natural looking? Impressive?

· Is the client fussy and demanding about workmanship, or will builder's standards be adequate?

· Is an open plan indicated or a series of clearly separated spaces?

· Are solar energy and design a factor?

· What furniture, art, equipment must be accommodated? What are future needs for these items?

· Is there an important indoor/outdoor relationship to nature or the street?

· How about resale or sublease? Is it realistic to design for unknown future inhabitants?

· Has maintenance been considered?

· Is there a desire or requirement for broad expanses of glass without mullions or smaller units that break up the walls and provide more enclosure? Is there a need for or objection to screens?

· What consideration has been given to both natural and artificial light? Which is preferable: a high level of lighting or subdued, restful levels? Are there specific activities that will require more light at times?

· Are there medical problems or code requirements for the handicapped to be considered?

· Is there some historical style, such as Colonial or Mission, that the client is enthusiastic about? A style the client doesn't like at all?

· Is a detail-oriented building with lots of nooks and crannies and idiosyncratic twists or a simple, straightforward plan desirable?

BUILDERS

· Has the builder worked with an architect before? Were there any problems?

· What aspects of the design look expensive?

· How detailed do the plans have to be?

· How often does the builder consult the architect? Is it better for the architect to call periodically?

· If the builder is the client for a multiple housing project, how many units will be built, based on how many models? What is the need for variations? How will you get paid: for the initial model or for subsequent replications?

· Is the builder willing to let the architect organize the team and select some suppliers or subcontractors?

· What system does the builder prefer to work with: lump sum contract based on plans and specifications? Direct costs plus a fixed profit amount? Other?

· Are there any problems with a lump sum contract arrangement? In inflationary times, for instance, there may be a system for the price of materials to be billed on a cost basis.

- Will the builder take the initiative to call the architect if he spots a detail that he thinks can be improved?

SITE

- What are the microclimatic conditions—sun, wind, temperature, humidity—of the site?

- Are there slopes and subsurface conditions to be taken into account?

- Is solar orientation possible and/or required?

- Is there a view to take advantage of or an unsightly one to avoid?

- Will a long access road be required?

- If a well is needed, how deep does it have to be? Will it be necessary to drill through rock? Should it be drilled with a rotary drill or "punched" with an up-and-down one?

- Is drainage adequate so that you can avoid building subsoil drainage systems?

- How far away are existing utility connections? Are there hookup charges?

- Are any erosion problems likely?

- Are there any ecological problems, such as contamination of nearby lakes and streams because of septic effluent?

- Is there likelihood of trapped ground water at any level that will cause problems with subsurface levels?

- Is the site in a Landmarks District that will require submission to and approval of an agency?

- Is there a design review board?

- What agencies require submittals for approval?

BUDGET

- Is the budget flexible?

- Has inflation been considered?

- Will the schedule affect costs?

- Has the cost of financing been figured and is it available?

- Will site conditions, such as the need for a well or long access road, affect costs? Have large items been budgeted separately? What about utility costs?

- Have first costs been balanced against operating costs for mechanical systems?

- What is included in the budget: just "bricks and mortar" or site development and utility costs as well? Have fees for lawyer, surveyor, and architect been budgeted separately?

- Is your fee to be settled initially, or will it be part of a flexible building budget?

- Where is the client's money coming from? Is most of it from the bank, and will that affect the contractor's payment schedule? Is any of the "up-front" money, such as your fee, to come from the bank? Does the client know that banks will lend money on a percentage of the total project, including fees and land?

- Is the land paid for?

- Are there any special procurement procedures for building the structure, such as friendly suppliers or subcontractors who will reflect the relationship with a low price?

THE ARCHITECT CAN COLLABORATE WITH THE CLIENT ON DESIGN DECISIONS

If the client is in one of the design professions or has past experience with building, the architect can set up a working relationship in which design decisions are made jointly. Here are two such examples.

If both client and architect share a common interest in some aspect of art, a joint search for items to include in the design can be fruitful and add to the client's sense of participation in the design process. The owner and architect selected old

building brackets that were incorporated by architect Arnold Syrop into decorative accents on interior columns of the Manhattan Ocean Club in New York City.

When the client works in the design field, work out a system of sharing design decisions through exchange of words or drawings. The graphic designer for whom this entrance lobby was designed had strong ideas concerning the visual image this space would project. As a result, architect Alfredo De Vido and artistic director Richard Moore of the graphics firm of Muir Cornelius Moore, Inc., exchanged ideas and reviewed each others' drawings.

DESIGN A COST-EFFECTIVE STRUCTURAL OR OTHER DESIGN DEVICE THAT WILL DOMINATE THE DESIGN CONCEPT

To solve a time or money problem, consider an overall concept to which other design decisions can be subordinated. This can take the form of a big prefabricated element, a single building material, a structural idea, a mechanical or light regulating system, or a dimensional module. Four examples are given below.

Consider the use of a major unifying element. The prefabricated roof of this house designed by Aldington, Craig and Collinge was transported 300 miles to the site in Devon, England, to solve a local labor and material problem.

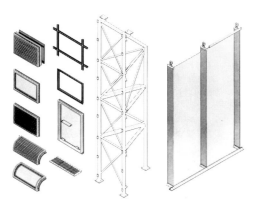

A need for light may suggest a unifying idea for the skin of the building. The need for open flexible space in this gallery in the Sainsbury Center for the Visual Arts in Norwich, England, required that natural lighting be regulated. The designed panel system enables any part of the external walls or roof to be changed to provide any combination of glazed, solid, or grilled aluminum panels. The project was designed by Foster Associates.

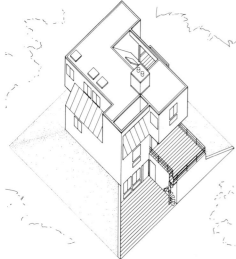

The use of a module can make complex spaces understandable to builders and clients. Carpenters were able to understand this combination of cubical forms by the use of a 3-foot 4-inch (102-cm) plan module and a builder's standard precut stud vertical module. These were used to build the Cohalan house in Bayport, New York, designed by Alfredo De Vido Associates

A single building material used throughout will lower costs and speed construction. The use of a local stone in this simple vacation house in Corsica enabled Roland Simounet to build the house in a short period at a cost below that of a prefabricated structure.

YOU CAN DESIGN WITH FEW DRAWINGS BY WORKING WITH VERNACULAR BUILDING TECHNIQUES

Building traditions are well entrenched throughout the world, because people working in the building trades tend to rely on materials and techniques they have experience with and those they know will do the job. Architects whose designs employ these traditions will accomplish their work with fewer communication problems with the builder and at generally lower costs, since builders can calculate costs more precisely when they understand the details. Examples of these vernacular traditions range from primitive mud building techniques still seen in Africa to sophisticated stone work in Germany. In the United States a well-established light wood framing tradition lets crews construct simple houses in a few weeks. Two examples follow.

The use of vernacular techniques does not restrict architects'

creativity. This Italian school in Broni near Pavia uses masonry construction common to many building types throughout Northern Italy. By careful placement of openings and the overall composition of the building, the architects have done an attractive building that is uncommon in its esthetic impact. Aldo Rossi and Gianni Bragheri were the architects.

Sometimes the best parts of a tradition can be adapted and prefabricated off site using manufactured components. In addition to a plan freely adapted from English Colonial traditions, architect John Andrews selected ordinary country building materials such as corrugated metal and showed in his home in Eugowra, Australia, that these could be combined with prefabricated elements available from manufacturer's catalogs to make appropriate house forms.

THOSE HAVING DIFFICULTY UNDERSTANDING DRAWINGS CAN LEARN FROM SIMPLE TIME-SAVING PRESENTATION TECHNIQUES

Most architects have had difficulty explaining their designs to some clients. Plan and section drawings are essential to architects, but can be incomprehensible to laypeople. A detailed model is frequently the answer, but these take time to build and are hard to modify. Axonometric drawings are useful, but their stiff geometries can be confusing. An alternative is the following technique:

A hybrid drawing/model technique can be used quickly and is widely

understandable. A drawing with depth to it like this one will enable non-architects to project themselves into the space and understand it more easily. This diorama of the Masterson Branch of the YWCA building in Houston, Texas, was produced by Taft Architects.

INCORPORATE ARTWORK INTO THE DESIGN OR DESIGN THE PROJECT AROUND A WORK OF ART

An architect may have special artistic talents or have a close working relationship with an artist. An integration of the structure with painting or sculpture can provide a focal point and add an additional dimension to the design, as shown in the following example.

Paint on a wall directly to provide interest to what might otherwise be uninviting surface. A trompe l'oeil painting at the end of a corridor leading to restrooms enlivens an otherwise unattractive dead end corridor in the restaurant Die Leiter in Frankfort, West Germany, designed by Jean-Pierre Heim of Design Connection International in Paris, France.

CRAFT ITEMS CAN ADD APPEALING HUMAN QUALITIES TO THE DESIGN

Some architects have, or know where to find someone with, handicraft abilities. It is possible to locate such things as specially made ceramic tiles, carefully wrought metalwork, or carved wood posts to give a unique handmade quality to the building. Here are two examples.

Stenciled floors are relatively inexpensive yet add rich pattern. A multicolored floor defines the public areas of the Springer Building in Galveston, Texas, and makes the act of entering this apartment building a special event. The renovation was by Taft Architects.

A unique cabinet reveals special care in design. The heart-shaped cutouts in this cabinet symbolize the affectionate family relationship of architect Louis Mackall and the owner, his sister Lucy Mackall. The house was built in Cambridge, Massachusetts.

A SYSTEMS APPROACH CAN SAVE MONEY AND MAKE THE DESIGN EASIER FOR OWNER AND BUILDER TO UNDERSTAND

Systems approaches have been used in the industrial world with varying success, often due to conservatism and fragmentation of the building industry. The systems have ranged from dimensional and computer-organized coordination of the drawings through total factory fabrication of units that are assembled on site. Two examples are shown below.

Total systems featuring on-site assembly of stock components offer variety in design. The assembly of metal components bolted together has long appealed to architects since it offers the possibility of flexible space arrangements using inexpensive industrial components. The T.E.S.T. System was put together by Helmut C. Schulitz.

A simple dimensional module can offer design legibility and cost savings. The plan and elevation modules used in this spatially complex house designed by Alfredo De Vido for Marylou Cohalan in Bayport, New York (see bottom of left column on page 29), enabled the carpenters to understand it easily. This in turn speeded their work and saved money.

THE ARCHITECT AS MASTER BUILDER OFFERS GREAT POTENTIAL

The elimination of "general" contractors can often produce quality construction faster and more economically. Most jobs are built by teams of specialists performing specific tasks such as carpentry, masonry, or sheet metal work. General contractors on small jobs often maintain their own crews, doing limited parts of the work and subcontracting the rest. On bigger jobs, general contractors will have only an administrative staff that will solicit bids, select subcontractors, and manage the work. These approaches have drawbacks, since the work is based on the architect's drawings and specifications, which can be misunderstood by those not familiar with them. If the architect serves as the organizer of the work, the chances for error or misinterpretation are lessened. This approach increases the work of the architect and his/her responsibilities. It assumes an organization capable of handling both functions, as in the following example.

Master building approaches require acceptance by all parties. Architects James Stirling and Michael Wilford worked within a system set up for multiple contracts on the Stuttgart Staatsgalerie in Stuttgart, West Germany. This enabled the job to be fast tracked economically.

THE ARCHITECT CAN INSIST ON THE EXECUTION OF HIS/HER DESIGN INTENT

In today's climate of collaboration on complex buildings, only a few architects are the final arbiters of their own designs. In the case of an architect with a distinctive design direction, clients generally acknowledge his/her lead in matters of esthetics. But usually they will insist that the budget and program be followed. Other consultants and trades are involved in the building during the planning and building stages. Therefore, to bring about the desired end result requires tenacity. Here's an example.

The final execution of early concepts requires careful and determined follow through. This stepped terrace was shown in its entirety on a drawing executed by the client for a vacation house in Provence in the early weeks of the design process. Roland Simounet was the architect.

SERVE AS THE DEVELOPER ON YOUR OWN DESIGNS

Architects are trained to organize. Since developers should be strong in organizational skills, it is possible that architects can also succeed as developers. They can see possibilities in a site or building that others could overlook. Also, architects will often know contractors capable of executing the design in a professional manner.

The major problem that architects must overcome is making design changes under construction. This can jeopardize the finances of the project. Another problem that can develop is architectural profit and loss versus development profit and loss. Ideally, both areas of work should be profitable and one should not underwrite the other. The possibilities of significant financial gain in a well-run development project far exceed the profit possibilities in a service-oriented profession. Here's an example.

Developing your own projects results in careful execution of the design intent. This final view of the building matches the early rendering prepared for a speculative commercial building in Houston, Texas. William T. Cannady was the architect.

CONSTRUCTION PHASES

Combining design with construction gives an opportunity to create better buildings more efficiently and at lower cost. The construction part of the process currently falls to general contractors or a professional managerial group. The American Institute of Architects (AIA) has recognized the trend toward new ways of practice and has produced Standard Forms of Agreements that spell out ways of working with or serving as the construction manager.

The architect's authority in interpreting the intent of the contract documents remains unchanged, but recommendations of the construction manager now play a more important part in determining means and techniques and dollar amounts due to contractors. Following are some alternate ways of handling construction.

BUILDING WITH YOUR OWN CREW WILL ENSURE CONTROL AND ENABLE YOU TO MAKE DESIGN DECISIONS DURING CONSTRUCTION

Some architects find they can achieve a richness of design and greater satisfaction from their work by building a significant portion of the work with their own construction crews. Most architect/builders who practice this way do minimal drawings, supplementing these with intensive design development under construction. They frequently have a budget, often tight, but manage to do a quality job due to their understanding and tailoring of the design intent. Most report a high level of job satisfaction from this kind of practice. Some have abandoned this approach due to either the time demands of construction work or greater workloads in the design setor. Three examples follow.

A complex shape is easier to build if the architect does it with own crew. Jersey Devil Design/Construction seeks to create a strong visual image on paper that will support job-site creativity for what is called the "airplane" house in Colorado City, Colorado.

Costs can be controlled if there is no wasted motion trying to under- stand architectural concepts. The lengths of the structural members were determined in on-site construction decisions. Acrylic glazing details were experimental and failed initially. Later correctional efforts were successful in the Barrett house in Damariscotta, Maine, designed and built by Sellers & Company.

Specialty items can be fabricated imaginatively. The kitchen cabinets and hood in the Lucy Mackall house in Cambridge, Massachusetts (see bottom of middle column on page 30), were built by Louis Mackall & Partner, Architects in their woodworking shop.

WHAT TO DO IF THE GENERAL CONTRACTOR DOESN'T WORK OUT ON A CONVENTIONAL ARRANGEMENT

1. Recognize the problem early. Discuss it frankly with your client. Find out if the client is willing to discharge the general contractor and take over the contractual relationship with, and payment of, the subcontractors.

2. If the client is willing to take over the job under your management, make a list of the subcontractors already on the job and which additional ones will be required. Talk to the ones on the job, explain what is happening, and ask if they will be willing to continue under your direction. Most will, since subcontractors are aware of developing job problems and will welcome direct payment by the owner, rather than run the risk of nonpayment by a defaulting contractor.

3. Review your time commitments and abilities to accomplish the additional work. If you are doubtful, don't attempt it. Project mangement requires enlightened leadership and the ability to insist that subcontractors meet their commitments.

4. Work out your fee arrangement with the owner. In a takeover effort when a contractor defaults, an hourly arrangement is recommended. You will not know how much time will be needed to sort out the problems. You also will not know who has been paid and what they have been told, and it may be necessary for you to arbitrate or make

a court appearance on behalf of the owner.

5. Lay out a time schedule for the balance of the work, adding 25 percent to your estimate. It will not be easy for you to coordinate all phases quickly, since you are coming into the management at midpoint and must have time to work out a relationship with new personnel.

Problems with a general contractor can lead to the following situation:

Failure to recognize contractor problems will result in extra job coordination for the architect. The contractor didn't understand the geometries of this greenhouse dining area in the Minton house in Copake, New York, designed by Alfredo De Vido Associates.

IF THE CLIENT IS IN THE CONSTRUCTION BUSINESS, CONSIDER WORKING AS A DESIGN CONSULTANT

It is unnecessary to perform full architectural services if your client is planning to perform the work with his own construction group. In such instances, the architect can limit his/her role to designing the building, outlining specs and details, establishing the design intent, and making submittals to proper agencies. It is important to make it clear to the client that consultation during the construction phase will ensure that the end product carries out the design intent. Here's an example.

The successful completion of a project done with a contractor or developer who is the owner will depend on his or her efforts as

Harris house in Los Angeles, California, for the owner.

much as the architect's. An important factor in the successful completion of this building at 222 Columbia Heights in Brooklyn, New York, was close cooperation between construction manager and architect Alfredo De Vido Associates.

IF YOU ARE SET UP FOR IT, DO THE WORK AS THE ARCHITECT AND THE CONSTRUCTION MANAGER

Although time consuming, a satisfying way of working is to arrange things so you take over as manager of construction. Some advantages to this are closer control of the execution of your design intent, a saving in time and money for the owner as well as earning more money for your own firm, and recognition of the greater responsibility and time commitment. There are disadvantages as well, such as potential legal liabilities, failure to meet deadlines, and overages on your budget. Given a good relationship with your client, the disadvantages can be explained and pitfalls minimized. But you must be careful to evaluate if you have the skills and the time to do this. Architecture and construction management are both full-time professions. This method of practice can work for isolated projects, but an active practice carried out entirely in this manner will require partners or key employees to share the workload. Whoever does the construction end of things must know how the industry operates. An example is given here.

Small projects are particularly suited to the architect's construction manager approach. To meet a tight budget, architect Rudolph M. Schindler subcontracted all aspects of the

THE OWNER MAY WANT TO SERVE AS THE GENERAL CONTRACTOR TO SAVE MONEY OR PARTICIPATE IN THE BUILDING PROCESS

If your clients express a desire to save money by eliminating the general contractor and doing the construction phase coordination themselves, you should ask them the following questions:

1. Do you have the time? About 10 hours a week might be the minimum required, assuming the subcontractors selected are reliable and can work independently.

2. Is your work close enough to the site to permit quick supervisory visits?

3. Are you able to budget your costs as you go along without adding extras along the way that will ultimately put total costs above the original budget?

4. Are you able to handle a crisis should one arrive, such as conflicting claims of subcontractors?

The architect should ask him/herself the following questions:

1. Do I have the time to devote to the extra amount of construction coordination that will be required? Have I worked out a fee arrangement to cover this time?

2. Is the owner committed to carry out the design intent of the drawings?

3. Is the owner qualified to serve as the general contractor, or will I be required to do the extra work?

If the answers to the questions indicate a favorable atmosphere for this method of

work, a carefully worked out written agreement documenting the roles of architect and owner is important. In it spell out what portion of your time under construction falls under normal architectural services and what portion to extra coordination as a result of the owner doing the job of the general contractor. Perhaps the best way is to bill all time in the construction phase as a separate service. The danger in this course is the owner's inclination to save on your fee by not calling you at all, in which instance the design intent may get diluted. An example follows.

Working with an owner who has had previous construction experience will make the job easier. The owner of the Cohalan house in Bayport, New York (see bottom of left column on page 29), designed by Alfredo De Vido Associates, had previous construction experience.

PERHAPS THE MOST SATISFYING ROLE FOR AN ARCHITECT IS TO SERVE AS ARCHITECT/CONTRACTOR/ OWNER

This approach enables the architect/manager/owner to decide what and how much money will be spent on design features and what the time schedule, fee structure, and profit margin will be. It means total control over the building process. Some questions should be asked:

1. Do I know enough to combine all these roles?

2. Am I able to order priorities sufficiently to permit a profitable end result?

3. Have I enough time, considering other work in the office?

4. Would it be more efficient and cost effective to hire a contractor, since he/she may be able to shop for prices more astutely?

5. Is there some technological problem that is best solved by this approach?

Perhaps the most important reason for combining all roles is the sense of accomplishment that will result in the end—the sense that you have created a building in all its aspects.

COMPENSATION

Innovative practice techniques require unusual fee arrangements. Architects can be compensated on a time, percentage, or fixed fee basis for any combination of work phases. They can also defer any payment until the building or buildings are sold or rented, speculating with their time and money in hope of greater financial reward than with conventional methods of practice.

As in any service industry, time is the basic commodity that any architect deals with. It is possible to sell this time in a package for which a lump sum of money is agreed upon beforehand or in a piece-meal fashion, billing as the work progresses and time is expended. A percentage basis relates the amount of compensation to the cost of the project. It doesn't recognize unusual circumstances or methods of practice that are not well defined. There are problems and benefits in any fee arrangement; six different methods are discussed below.

TIME

Time compensation is a safe and equitable way to perform professional services. It assumes a climate of trust between client and professional and an efficient service organization. Most clients will ask for a rough estimate of total costs before agreeing to this means of billing for required services. It is important for the architect to continuously update his/her time estimates and let the client know how much time has accrued and why original targets have been exceeded if they have. Failure to keep the client advised of accruing costs may result in serious misunderstandings and endanger the project.

PERCENTAGES

Percentages, the time-honored method of practice, is possibly the most misleading and confusing method of compensation, particularly when designing smaller projects such as houses, stores, and offices. The chief fault with this method is its failure to relate the scope of services to the cost of the project. For example,

some scopes require the production of preliminary drawings with rudimentary contract documents and minimal supervision. Comparing this with extensive design/management services is misleading and inequitable. It is also exceedingly difficult to explain to a client who has heard that the "usual" percentage arrangement is 10 percent.

FIXED FEES

A fixed fee arrangement generates a sense of security at the beginning of a project. Clients feel they have started the project with a sound grasp on the overall costs; the architect views the sum of money as equal to the task. If the architect has been through the process many times, he or she will be able to estimate the time required accurately and come up with a fixed fee that is sufficient enough to cover costs and overhead, plus reasonable profit. Prior knowledge or a previous working relationship with the client will help the architect gauge costs even more accurately. However, unfamiliarity with the task or client may result in serious cost overruns that may make the architect lose money or cut back on the amount of service required in order to avoid losses. Either course will be unsatisfactory professionally, financially, and emotionally for both client and architect.

SPECULATION

Due to the risks involved, speculation should be the most remunerative means of practice. It presupposes sufficient financial reserves to carry the cost of producing the service documents and, in the case of speculative building, the cost of producing the actual building or buildings. It should never be undertaken if there are any questions in the architect's mind about the financial viability of the project or the credit worthiness of the client. The architect must also bear in mind that any request for him to speculate with his services is equivalent to a request to speculate with his money. Careful evaluation is essential.

A MIXTURE OF METHODS

Fixed or percentage fees for design/contract documents and time for programming or construction services is one example of how different methods can be combined. Since it is possible for architects to closely monitor time spent producing sketches, models, and drawings (as they are not so dependent on the work or input of others), a fixed or percentage fee for this portion of the work can be equitable to all parties. Programming, including site selection, and construction services involve others whose work productivity or ability to produce answers are difficult to estimate unless the architect has worked with the parties before. A combination of these two arrangements is easier to explain to the client, since the difficulty of gauging others' time is apparent. Even conventional contracts provide for extra compensation if construction time is exceeded.

ANOTHER COMBINATION OF METHODS

Fixed or percentage fees plus speculative or bonus sums for successful or profitable completion of the project is another possible combination. Assuming coverage of the architect's costs and overhead, a profit-sharing or bonus arrangement can give added incentives to the architect and make the owner feel that the architect will do his/her best to ensure a successful project. The amount and payment time of such arrangements should be carefully spelled out. Failure to do so will result in misunderstandings. Remember, and try to explain, that the financial or esthetic success of a project depends on the quality of the services provided, rather than on a simple multiplier of hours. An esthetically pleasing shopping center or housing group can result in high sales or rental income far exceeding normal expectations. It is not unreasonable for the architect to share in these rewards.

Many combinations of fee arrangements are possible. The key ingredient is mutual trust between architect and client.

CASE STUDIES

The work of the various architects in the book was solicited after a review of, and as a result of conversations on, design and management techniques prevalent in the United States and abroad. Although this survey is not exhaustive, it represents the broad possibilities available to the practitioner. The quality of visual material and written descriptions vary according to the nature of the approach. For example, builder/architects do not do a lot of drawings or verbally explain their work—they simply build. Others, such as Foster Associates in England, make extensive use of drawings, sketches, and models to explain and build their ideas, and this is reflected in the quantity of their material presented here.

The procuring of the material was easy for work that was well documented. However, in other instances, data and documentation required considerable effort, thereby accounting for the varying amounts of material on different projects.

Projects are prefaced by an introduction to the firm's general design approach. Then a box lists the project's description, location, architect, and date of completion, and there is a brief discussion of the particular project's background. Four categories of information are always included: A Design Features section describes unique spaces, geometries, colors, or other aspects of the design. A Design/Manage Technique section identifies those management ideas that are the chief concern of this book. Cost Control notes how the design/manage techniques affect costs, and Schedule describes any unusual time factors.

R. M. SCHINDLER
(1887–1953)
Los Angeles, California

Leading California pioneer adapted personal beliefs to emerging local building technology

Almost all of R. M. Schindler's buildings were built with Schindler himself serving as director of the subcontractors. He journeyed to job sites in a car laden with tools and building materials and spent much of his time there. His assistants (when he had them) were instructed to draw rough sketches. Then he would work out final details on site with the carpenters and masons.

Techniques of construction and unusual applications of current building methods interested Schindler. For example, he did not care for the onionlike layering of materials normally used in house construction and experimented with concrete and wood frames infilled with glass or insulating material. He experimented with movable forms for concrete, expressing the horizontal pour lines after the forms had been removed. Other explorations included sprayed concrete, concrete block, and earthquake-proof construction through the use of rigid concrete frames, as in the Lovell beach house.

R. M. Schindler, born in Vienna in 1889, came to the United States at the age of 27 in the hope of studying with Frank Lloyd Wright. He worked with Wright at Taliesin on the Imperial Hotel in Tokyo until Wright took him to Los Angeles to work on the Olive Hill project, a cultural center for Hollywood. The center was to contain a house for the client, a theater, other houses, studio apartments for artists, and a group of stores. During much of the time Olive Hill was under construction, Wright was in Japan working on the hotel, leaving Schindler to cope with the complexities of construction and budget, as well as the irritation of the owner. It was during this period that Schindler gained the experience handling construction problems that proved invaluable to him in his later independent practice.

By 1920, Schindler left Wright's firm; work there had dwindled. He had given up on the idea of returning to Vienna, which had become architecturally and politically conservative, and he found the Los Angeles area congenial to his new ideas. In 1921, he built a two-family house on King's Road, which he shared with the engineer Clyde Chase. It served as the base of operations for most of his professional life.

Despite his early training under Wright, Schindler evolved a personal style based loosely on de Stijl, the Dutch Expressionist movement. Volume and space were his interest as early as 1912, as noted in his *A Manifesto*. He gradually discarded Wright's design vocabulary and worked with compositions of surfaces and volumes. He also departed from the bold use of color after the de Stijl architects as his palette became more muted.

He believed in his abilities as an artist, although he tried to improve his public image by taking an interest in the mechanics and practicalities of building. He pioneered in the use of the 4-foot (122-cm) module, claiming it saved time and money, while permitting design flexibility. His late 1930s houses also revealed the influence of the International Style, as practiced in California at that time by Richard J. Neutra, Raphael Soriano, and J. R. Davidsc

Modular techniques and construction management applied to tiny hillside house

Project: *Rose Harris house, Los Angeles, California*
Architect: *Rudolph M. Schindler*
Date Completed: *1942*

Designed in 1942 and built in compliance with the Defense Housing Restrictions of that time, this small Schindler house was sited on a rocky ridge. Its placement provided unobstructed views from all rooms and also allowed garage space to be located below the main living level.

When the contract was signed with the architect in March 1942, speed of execution was important to the client because of her health problems. She therefore asked if foundations could be poured prior to the completion of the design. While Schindler's reply is unknown, his drawings look hastily prepared and include only ¼-inch (6-mm) scale plans, elevations, and interior sections. Few details are shown on the drawings, but Schindler frequently worked out details on site with the builder, and some correspondence indicates that the builder may have been the client's brother, facilitating such an informal arrangement.

Two complete sets of drawings survive, one for a 660-square-foot (61-square-meter) house that includes a nook off the living room, and one for a 590-square-foot (55-square-meter) house with the nook deleted and with a smaller bedroom. The smaller version was built, presumably for budgetary reasons.

DESIGN FEATURES

Time constraints, a tight budget, and Schindler's unusual working methods determined the management of this job.

The house had a concrete foundation following the contours of the rock outcropping, a wood frame, and gray-green stucco with wood trim to match. Custom-fixed and operable windows were provided. Interior wood was stained to match the exterior. Interior stucco was greenish yellow. Wall-to-wall carpeting in similar tones completed the scheme.

The stucco walls are fitted into the rock outcropping in the Harris house.

Schindler made the small house appear larger by positioning the pergola extension on the rock outcropping.

Small spaces are made to look larger in the Harris house by built-ins and the positioning of the windows.

DESIGN/MANAGE TECHNIQUES

Schindler handled all the work personally. The architect signed a standard AIA Form of Agreement on a fee basis of 10 percent of the cost of construction.

The house has been destroyed, but photos show that it was built in accordance with the drawings. Later correspondence dated 1947 with the same client who was then considering a speculative house in Palm Springs indicated that the architect was outspoken in his recommendations to clients. Mrs. Harris was contemplating being her own builder for this new venture. Schindler's reply is unequivocal: "Considering your nature, your pocketbook and your health, I do not think the strain on all of them would be worth the gain you can make. Building at the present time taxes the professional, but for the layman it is murder."

COST CONTROL

According to Julius Shulman, the photographer who took the pictures of this house, Schindler would price out his work, calling individual subcontractors and material suppliers and asking the price of the various quantities to be installed. If the totals were beyond the budget, he would redesign.

SCHEDULE

Projected actual time schedules are undocumented.

The semicurcular fireplace is integrated with the built-in sofa.

Right: Schindler was careful to note the contour of the land in the plan for the Harris house.

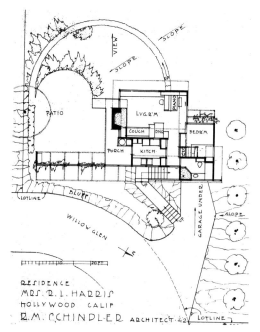

RESIDENCE
MRS. R. L. HARRIS
HOLLYWOOD CALIF
R.M. SCHINDLER ARCHITECT 42

Architect builds own house

Project: *Schindler/Chase house, Los Angeles, California*
Architect: *Rudolph M. Schindler*
Date Completed: *1921*

Schindler used his own house as a vehicle for many spatial and technical ideas. The house was planned for use by four adults, the Schindlers and the Chases (Chase was Schindler's engineer). A cooperative house was built on a small lot incorporating four studios, since Schindler believed that everyone needs a place of his or her own. Each pair of 16- × -24-foot (5- × -7-meter) studios forms an L around a patio, closed off in the winter by canvas sliding doors. To these interior and exterior rooms, an arrangement of hedges and trees was added, dividing the lot into many outdoor zones.

The layout was a radical break from traditional plans of that time, particularly since there were no bedrooms. Instead, narrow stairs led to sheltered roof decks, where residents were to sleep in the open. This design ignored the winter climate of Los Angeles, which is sometimes cold and rainy, and the decks were later closed in. The house otherwise incorporated many concepts that have since become part of California living—such as the narrow wings around a patio, slab floors continuous with outdoor spaces, clerestory lighting, and nonbearing sliding partitions.

Exterior courts are defined by the wings of the house built for Schindler and his engineer Chase.

Interiors show how the tie beams extend between the exterior precast panels and the glass wall.

Above: Slits of light mark the divisions in the tilt-up concrete wall.

Left: Sliding glass walls open the interior to the garden courts.

DESIGN FEATURES

In addition to the unusual planning concepts and the owner-built construction, there were other out of the ordinary aspects to the house, such as slab on grade construction with tilt-up concrete walls at edges; modular construction; integration of landscape with interiors; and exposure of structural materials.

DESIGN/MANAGE TECHNIQUES

The design incorporated a number of prefabrication ideas, such as the tilt-up wall slabs. These were made on the floor slab to dimensions of 8′ 6″ × 3′ 9″ (3 × 1 m) and given textural interest by membranes laid previously on the slab. These membranes, which prevented adhesion of the wall units to the floor, were of three types: soft soap directly on the slab to produce a smooth finish, Kraft paper to produce a wrinkled finish, and burlap bags for a canvaslike finish. The tilt slabs were tapered from 9½″ (24 cm) at the bottom to 5″ (13 cm) at the top. They were infilled with glass 3″ (8 cm) wide, grouted at top and bottom, and joined with a wooden bond beam bolted through at the top. This construction was innovative for the time, and early construction photos show workers tilting the heavy slabs into place with simple block and tackle.

Other details in the house include modular stud placement 2 feet (61 cm) on center and a stock horizontal member notched into these to take infill material. These were prefabricated to a T shape and intended to speed assembly and cut costs by serving as structural members and finish pieces at the same time. These trim pieces were infilled with glass or ½″ (1.3-cm) thick composition board.

Plumbing was arranged in a sculptural way and left exposed, and lighting consisted of bulbs fitted between exposed beams and covered by frosted glass slipped into place.

COST CONTROL

Since Schindler served as his own contractor, costs were kept economical.

SCHEDULE

The basic shell of the house was built in 1921. Modifications and embellishments to the building were made throughout Schindler's residence there.

ALDINGTON, CRAIG AND COLLINGE

Partners: Peter Aldington, John Craig, Paul Collinge
Haddenham Bucks, England

Structural systems provide framework for free planning

The work of Aldington, Craig and Collinge is diversified among residential and institutional buildings, such as post offices and the health care center shown on pages 46–48.

The firm is composed of eight architects plus eight other staff, with the design emphasis provided mainly by partners Peter Aldington and Paul Collinge. Their design direction is marked by strongly expressing structure and materials. In their plans, they prefer forms containing single-purpose rooms surrounded by multipurpose community or family social areas.

The process by which most of the firm's buildings are put up follows the nature of the structural system and includes use of uniform stopping points for materials. This helps give the builder the sense of the order of the design and in turn helps the building be erected rapidly with greater economy.

However, the architects believe strongly that systems cannot be set up that will enable unskilled craftsmen to achieve high-quality results. They think that unless a good number of the many factors that go into the making of a building are in the architect's favor, high-quality buildings will not result.

Prefabricated roof system trucked 300 miles to remote site

Project: *House, Devon, England*
Architects: *Aldington, Craig and Collinge*
Date Completed: *1971*

Aldington, Craig and Collinge were commissioned by a professional man to design a house for his family of three in the Devon countryside. The site had a fine view and rooms were to be planned to take advantage of it. Other requirements were a living room and kitchen, both as spacious as possible; a small dining area; three bedrooms; and a study close to the living areas, with its clutter concealed from view.

This overall view of the house in Devon, England, shows the rectangular roof supported on columns over freely placed elements below.

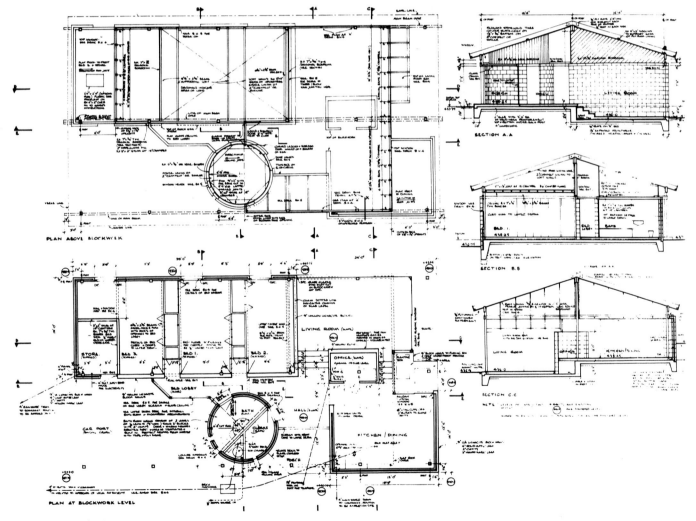

Plans indicate a loose grouping of elements below the roof.

Study area on far left is enclosed by a low masonry wall to conceal work in progress yet provide openness within the room.

DESIGN FEATURES

The study—an open alcove in which the professional can work and still be part of his family's life—is designed so any untidiness in the workspace is screened off.

The roof plane seems to float above the spaces below, due to the glazed gable ends and a thin clerestory strip of glass running the length of both sides of the building. The bedroom area is enclosed with concrete block, while the loft storage area is located between the ceiling and the roof.

DESIGN/MANAGE TECHNIQUES

The architects' office was located 300 miles (483 kilometers) from this remote site, to which transportation was difficult. This prompted the architects to design a prefabricated roof system to be constructed near their Oxford offices under their supervision, transported to the site, and erected by a local builder. The roof design of 1760 square feet (164 square meters) was considerably larger than the floor area of 1405 square feet (131 square meters) to provide generous overhangs and sheltered patio areas. This also gave the architects the advantage of a simple, economical roof system under which more complex shapes, such as the circular bathroom group, could be located.

The prefabricated roof, with its post-and-beam supports, is clearly seen inside and out because of the glazed separation of the exterior walls from the roof and the dark stain of the structural posts. Structural order is carried into the blockwork as well, which is stopped at a uniform height throughout the house.

A percentage of the construction costs was charged for the architects' fee. There were no extra fees for the design of built-in furniture or other aspects of interior design that the architects handled, such as the choice of curtains or the selection of loose furniture.

COST CONTROL

The prefabricated roof structure, even with the added cost of transportation and a higher labor cost due to off-site construction, cost no more than a completely site-fabricated house. In return, the owners and architects got a house tailored to their requirements with a consistently high level of workmanship. Careful dimensional coordination was possible, and any tendency on the part of the local builder to take license with the design was restricted by the prefabricated roof structure.

SCHEDULE

The house was built in seven months, a reasonable time for a house. This indicated that the off-site fabrication of the roof didn't delay construction.

The roof is supported at the ridge by free-standing columns.

Flexible plan fits health center

Project: *North Woolwich Health Center, London, England*
Architects: *Aldington, Craig and Collinge*
Date Completed: *1980*

The problem confronting the architects here was to design a building containing a number of identical clinical rooms of a given size and shape in which privacy and confidentiality were to be preserved. These rooms were to be served by a reception/administration area from which a waiting area could be controlled and supervised, with access to staff areas.

A further consideration in planning the building was that the site—560 square meters (2009 square feet) including garden courtyards—was in a noisy, declining area of London, where vandalism was rampant. Construction was to proceed rapidly, according to the owner's schedule.

DESIGN FEATURES

Partition systems, furniture, and plug-in units can be placed and rearranged under a lightweight prefabricated steel roof structure. Consulting rooms look into small courtyards, relieving the eye with greenery in this bleak urban area. An extensive system of skylights provides natural light within the building, since exterior walls are mostly blank and solid for security.

Interiors are consciously designed to look domestic through the scale of the rooms, color—largely greens and yellows—and an airy, light feeling.

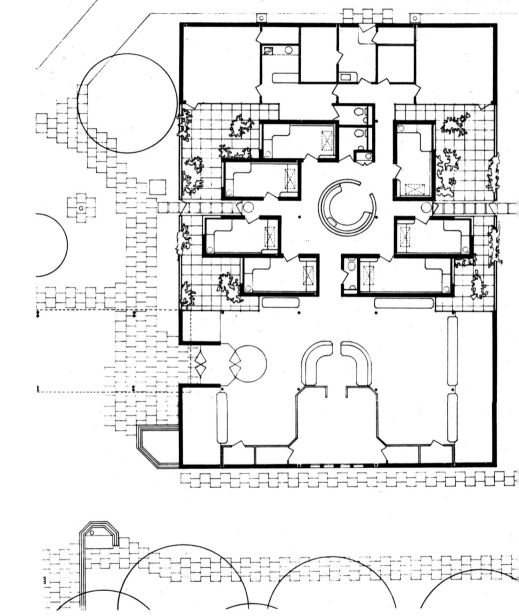

A cluster of examination rooms is at the center of a walled rectangle in the North Woolwich Health Center.

DESIGN/MANAGE TECHNIQUES

The requirement for rapid construction suggested a roof structure that could be erected early so work could go on in bad weather. The architects therefore designed a lightweight steel structure covered with roof planking. The site contained unstable soil and demanded a structure capable of support by a concrete slab foundation resting on the ground. The architects designed the structure with closed concrete block walls and spaces that looked into the courtyards or were toplit.

The construction techniques adopted also fit the owner's call for quick erection, turning this potential problem into an environmental benefit by creating an inward-looking but well-lit series of spaces. The architects did not receive any additional fees for their design approach or the design of built-in furniture.

The key process involved in this project was the designers' close study of the program requirements. They worked out a series of diagrams illustrating the complex demands of doctors treating patients and the circulation of patients within the building for treatment and nursing services. As a result of this analysis, the plan reveals boxlike consulting rooms arranged around the nurses' area. Secondary services, such as storage areas, are immediately adjacent to this central area and reached by a short corridor.

Above: The exterior of the health center is surrounded by masonry walls to provide security.

Left: Peaked skylights provide not only required drainage but design interest.

COST CONTROL

Budget estimates for the work were met.

SCHEDULE

The unusual construction approach dictated by the design was intended to speed construction. Unfortunately it had the reverse effect because the builder was not used to an unconventional approach. Since the job was a public structure, the architects were required to take the low bidder and had no control over the choice of contractors.

The open plan within the health center shows light entering from skylights at the perimeter of the rooms.

Exterior enclosed garden courts provide views from the rooms within.

DESIGN CONNECTION INTERNATIONAL

Jean-Pierre Heim, Architect
Paris, Milan, New York

Systematic marketing approach increases scope of architect's services

Design Connection International offers a complete range of services to Paris-based businesses for establishing overseas commercial enterprises. Jean-Pierre Heim, an architect trained at the École des Beaux-Arts, has both an artistic and a business background. He has organized groups of realtors, marketing analysts, graphic artists, attorneys, engineers, and code expediters in three major cities. Excerpts from his 1983 lecture to the French Chamber of Commerce, which are reprinted here, are an example of his approach to the U.S. market. Note the way he stresses the practical realities of designing stores:

DEVELOPMENT OF THE PROJECT

The choice of a site is of primary importance to good marketing and a successful commercial enterprise. The two strategic areas for commercial development in the United States are downtown and the suburban shopping malls. "Downtown" is the commercial center consisting of office buildings, banks, shops, and churches. Shopping malls are a development of the American suburb and are large covered spaces containing a number of stores.

ROLE OF THE ARCHITECT

It is practically impossible for the owner to open a store on a do-it-yourself basis in the United States. To arrange all the various elements and secure the necessary permits would be an unproductive use of time and energy.

Drawings and documents are required for any alterations. These must be prepared by a registered architect or engineer. The role of the architect, interior designer, or engineer is to prepare sketches and contract drawings, submit them to the client, and supervise their execution after the necessary permits are secured. Depending upon the scope of the work, health, electrical, plumbing, fire department, and HVAC permits must be obtained. The professional assumes the responsibility of guiding the project through these channels.

Several steps are required to get started. First of all, a site must be selected. It is advisable to consult with a specialist on this matter. Once a location is chosen, it is necessary to obtain a lease from the proprietor. This should be reviewed by a lawyer.

Then it will be necessary to have a sign made up to advertise the name and type of the establishment. The name should be easy to pronounce in English. A building permit must be obtained before construction is started. The permit application must include complete architectural and engineering data. Drawings must be filed with the Building Department in conformity with their regulations. A Certificate of Occupancy will be required to reflect the new use and number of people using the establishment. Inspectors from the Building Department will inspect the work at critical intervals for all HVAC, fire, health, and structural areas of the work. In some special cases it may be necessary to secure the approval of a Landmarks or Fine Arts Commission. Delays on the construction site are possible if engineering details are not reviewed and accepted by the inspectors.

Bids should be solicited from three general contractors and the results evaluated by the architect and client. The contract should be reviewed by an attorney.

When selecting the general contractor it is necessary to determine whether he is capable of completing the required work to the client's satisfaction, whether his labor is union or nonunion (which can be a cost factor), and whether he has the proper insurance.

Average prices for construction range from $30 to $100 per square foot. Procurement time is an important factor to keep in mind, particularly in the New York region. Furniture should be selected from in-stock items, since delays of 16 or more weeks can be experienced. The typical schedule for completion of a store or commercial office will be from four to six months. Two months will be required for the architectural and engineering drawings, two weeks for the solicitation of bids, and two to four months for the actual construction.

ARCHITECTURE AND THE FACADE

The architecture and the facade should reflect the character of the product to be sold. There are three types of storefronts: the facade of a new free-standing building, those that are part of a longer group of stores, and corner facades. These various types require different design solutions.

The design of the interiors is also an important adjunct to the display and selling of the product. The store window should be designed to draw attention to the presentation of the products. Frequently changing merchandise in the store windows is desirable to keep the product image fresh.

In franchise operations where there is more than one commercial outlet for the same product, a visual identity is important and should be carried through in the facades, signage, logo, announcements, packaging, and documents.

Publicity is useful in launching a new store. A public relations firm can be retained to draw attention to the opening through the media.

Through presentations of this type, Heim conveys his firm's capabilities to a wide range of French entrepreneurs wishing to open a branch overseas. Once he is retained as architect, it is possible for Heim to locate space, assess its commercial possibilities, review technicalities and legal problems, and make an architectural presentation to business executives in Paris. This comprehensive scope of services is valuable, and Design Connection International has succeeded in expanding its market as a result of this strategy.

Architect executes theatrical theme, contracts out specialty items

Project: *Die Leiter, Frankfurt, West Germany*
Architects: *Jean-Pierre Heim, Design Connection International*
Date completed: *November 1982*

A theatrical atmosphere has been created for this restaurant in a long narrow space on a pedestrian street near the Frankfurt Opera in the theater district. The name chosen for the restaurant, "Die Leiter," which means "the ladder" in German, was selected because it is a symbol of cinematic scenery. This symbol is found in the neon signage, calling cards, and menus of the restaurant. It is prominently displayed in red neon on the back of the bar and in the rear of the restaurant in a trompe l'oeil painting. The theme is further reinforced by an actual ladder near the entrance, which daring patrons can climb to locate their friends or make their presence known.

The cinematic image is reinforced by five projectors that show scenes on the back wall and a band of blackboard painted to look like 35mm film on which the day's menu is chalked. On each table a box of crayons enables patrons to sketch on the paper tablecloths, if they wish.

The space is lively, with a checkered diagonal floor in two shades of marble, a bar front composed of marble tile and brick in an irregular pattern, and a back bar of glass block backlit to feature bottles displayed in front of it. A pipe scaffold hung from the ceiling has theatrical lights clamped to it, and two overhead ceiling fans provide necessary air movement, along with ventilators to clear the smoke. Two Ionic columns made of papier-mâché add a whimsical touch. One runs from the bar top to the ceiling, while the other is fragmented at the bottom and hung simply from the ceiling.

The restaurant and bar take up 1200 square feet (112 square meters), while the kitchen is 350 square feet (33 square meters).

Trompe l'oeil painting at the end of the restroom corridor enlivens an otherwise dead end in the Frankfurt restaurant.

The exterior of the restaurant can be opened to provide a glimpse of the interior.

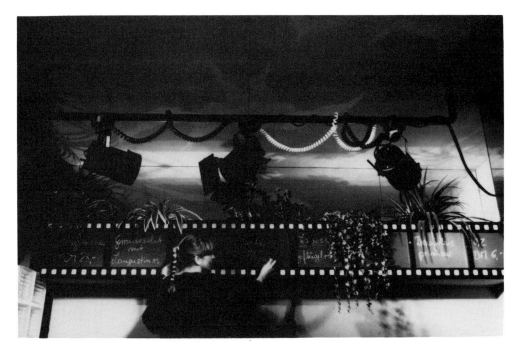

Menus are written in chalk on the cinematic strip above the bar.

This view is taken from the summit of the ladder at the entrance.

DESIGN FEATURES

The design reflects a collage approach to assembling the various elements. It was the design intent to create a sense of the changing atmosphere of a cinematic theme. Heim personally executed the ladder mural at the rear of the restaurant in the hall and obtained the papier-mâché columns and film projectors from New York.

DESIGN/MANAGE TECHNIQUES

The architect included all items on the contract documents that were necessary for the building permit, contracting separately for specialty items such as the theatrical lighting, the bar, and built-in and movable seating.

The architect personally supervised the arrangement of important visual elements such as the glass block at the back of the bar, the fragmented brick and marble tile front bar, and the placement of the papier-mâché columns and entrance ladder.

Fifteen percent was charged for architectural services. The mural was painted for an agreed-upon lump sum. Specialty items such as the columns and the projectors were purchased by the architect for the owner for an agreed-upon sum, with an administrative markup of 15 percent.

COST CONTROL

The basic interior finishes were simple and easily priced by the contractors. All unusual items were procured separately, thereby lowering costs, since all items are usually included under one contract. Ordering these items separately also ensured their timely arrival.

SCHEDULE

There were no unusual time constraints, other than the customary desire of commercial clients to occupy their space as soon as possible.

New studio restores and enhances 17th-century mansion

Project: *Studio de Production Costa Renouf, Paris, France*
Architects: *Jean-Pierre Heim, Design Connection International*
Date completed: *February 1983*

When the architect was engaged to design this project in the historic Marais district of Paris, the existing space in the building was cluttered and somber, show-ing the wear and tear of time. Mouldings and cornices of the walls and ceilings had been damaged and covered with many coats of paint.

The client, a producer of advertising films, wished to divide the 1200-square-foot (112-square-meter) reception room into three zones: an entry reception area, a bar for serving refreshments, and an area for screening films.

The logo of the Paris firm is displayed in neon behind the hospitality bar.

Concurrent design/construction transforms abandoned building

Project: *Mercantile Building, Scranton, Pennsylvania*
Architects: *Leung Hemmler Camayd, P.C.*
Date Completed: *1982*

A private, profit-making partnership was formed in June 1982 to eliminate blighted areas in downtown Scranton. A dilapidated and abandoned structure called the Mercantile Building was undertaken as its first endeavor, which became the first major renovation project in the city in many years.

The architects were asked to transform the 15,200-square-foot (1412-square-meter) building into an attractive, well-appointed structure to house high-quality retail tenants on the ground floor and provide professional office space on the upper two floors. When initially approached in June 1982, the architects realized that the time allotted for the renovation would be the major challenge. The prime prospective tenant was a gift shop, and it was essential to have commercial space completed on the first floor prior to the Christmas shopping season. Time available for construction was therefore less than four months. Determined to help downtown revitalization, the architects committed considerable resources to accomplish the task.

The rehabilitated building now houses the gift shop, a ladies' wear boutique, a quality men's clothing store, and a florist on the ground floor, and office space is being developed for the upper stories. A glass canopy was used to transform the entire first floor facade into one large display window, and classical design elements were located to mark store entrances and complement the original facade. The renovated building serves to add new commercial life to downtown Scranton.

The entire ground floor of the Mercantile Building is surrounded by a greenhouse structure to provide visability and display for the new shops.

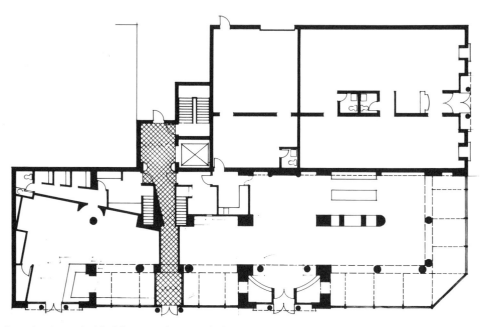

Round columns behind the greenhouse exterior support the existing building above.

New features clearly mark the entrance and recall detail of the earlier building.

DESIGN FEATURES

Design decisions were shaped by two primary considerations. First, the ground floor was structurally unsound, so it was imperative to design foundation supports to give stability to the old structure. Second, because this street corner had been abandoned for so many years, a dramatic visual effect was needed on the ground level to transform the entire image of the area.

Both these considerations were solved by designing new masonry entrances to provide structural support as well as visual continuity with architectural elements on the upper levels. A large glass canopy along the entire expanse of the ground floor transformed the commercial space into one large display window.

DESIGN/MANAGE TECHNIQUES

When the owner came to the architects, he had already selected a contractor, who, although he had little experience with restoration work of this scale or complexity, was able to adjust to the demands of the job, thanks to a good working relationship with both the owner and the architects.

From the beginning, the architects enjoyed the confidence of the owner/developer and were consulted at all critical points. The initial phase of the project absorbed the entire firm. For two weeks all six architects were involved in a crash program that included detailed survey work, basic building measurements, initial design plans, zoning approvals, bid solicitations, and coordination work with engineers. Throughout the project, design and construction proceeded simultaneously, necessitating daily phone calls and site meetings at least three times a week for one architect. Considerable overtime, plus the addition of some temporary freelance professionals, was necessary to meet office commitments.

The architects worked closely with both the glass manufacturer and the local installer to ensure satisfactory installation of the large expanse of glass used for the canopy. It was an unusual experience for the firm to work with both the owner/developer and the prospective tenants at the same time. As intermediary between these two parties, they had to devise new office guidelines to meet the needs of both.

Fees were set at 8 percent of the original construction bid plus an hourly charge for any additional work. However, because of the many complex problems encountered during the hectic building process, the "additional work" became a part of the daily construction work. Although this extra time was considerable, the firm's final billing did not exceed the original 8 percent. The architects believe the experience and the visibility they gained from this important urban project supplemented the modest fee.

COST CONTROL

Because of the unique aspects of this project and of time constraints, cost control was difficult. There was insufficient time for thorough planning and analysis prior to the construction phase, and unanticipated structural problems occurred, requiring additions and changes during construction.

The cost overrun was close to 15 percent, due mainly to the short construction time and the nature of renovation work.

SCHEDULE

The architects managed to meet a difficult three-month time schedule from design to completion of the commercial space. The gift shop opened October 15, as planned, in time for the Christmas season.

Details within the shops are integrated with the old exterior.

Architect is designer/contractor for own house

Project: *Camayd house, Clark Summit, Pennsylvania*
Architect: *Leung Hemmler Camayd, P.C.*
Date Completed: *January 1983*

The basic design of the Camayd house was strongly influenced by the 2400-square-foot (223-square-meter) lot. Surrounded by many tall trees, this pocket of land had been cleared by the previous owner. The architect therefore decided to take advantage of the open space by transforming it into a large flower garden and designing the house to overlook it.

The entrance on the north side leads to a foyer flanked by a colonnade that cuts through and extends beyond the house to frame the garden. This axis is an important design feature; other spaces become incidental to this path. Large windows fronting the garden unify the various areas into an open living space. The garden acts as a buffer, protecting the house from the street and neighboring homes.

DESIGN FEATURES

Classical influences and axial relationships give the house an imposing presence. Inventiveness is apparent in the details. The horizontal rustications are marble scraps cut into strips and inlaid in the colored stucco surface. The oversized columns on the garden side support "transparent" steel brackets that hold the green wisteria canopy. In contrast with the large windows below, those on the second floor are small punctures in the solid mass. This juxtaposition thereby creates an illusion of imposing size in what is a small informal house.

The plan of the Camayd house is rectangular, enlivened by extensions and oversized piers.

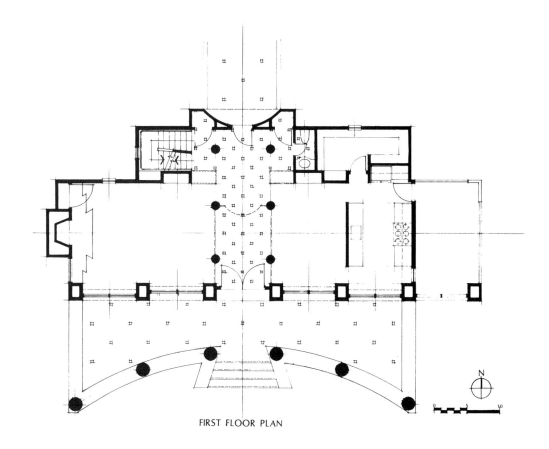

FIRST FLOOR PLAN

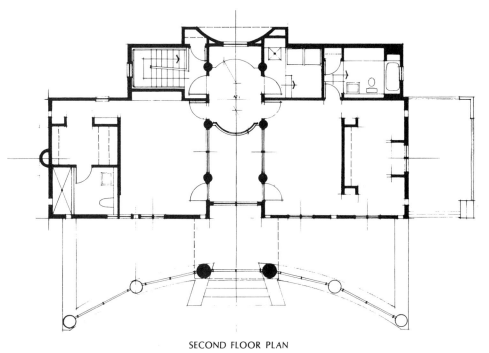

SECOND FLOOR PLAN

Right: Overscaled columns are combined with light metal trusses to give a large scale to the garden facade.

Below: A peaked free-standing column at the end of the side deck both extends and terminates the house.

Etched glass, paned doors, patterned vinyl tile floors, and color enliven the view toward the garden.

DESIGN/MANAGE TECHNIQUES

The architect served as designer and general contractor for his house. Office critiques of the design were solicited periodically.

In the course of construction, the architect experimented with several custom-made items. Coordinating the work of local craftsmen with that of the basic subcontractors necessitated special arrangements for execution and installation. Because of the extra effort required by this coordination, the architect's time spent on the site was far greater than that for most residential projects.

Architectural fees were not an issue for this house. However, the question of contractors' fees was a relevant concern. While avoiding the 10 to 15 percent additional cost of a general contractor, the architect had to invest valuable professional time in his own project.

COST CONTROL

In an effort to contain costs, the architect assumed the job as general contractor. This became a problem due not only to his inexperience as a general contractor but to the time that he was required to spend away from his regular practice. The actual net cost benefits of this arrangement were difficult to assess, since the architect and his wife decided that they were less willing to sacrifice design and material quality to achieve cost savings than the average client.

SCHEDULE

There was little deviation from the projected six-month building schedule.

ALFREDO DE VIDO ASSOCIATES, ARCHITECTS
New York, New York

Office systems, multiple contracts used to control quality at lower cost

While Alfredo De Vido Associates, Architects do not limit the firm's practice to small projects, these provide a steady source of work. Since clients for these projects do not usually come with high budgets, it has been necessary for the architect to evolve ways of meeting budgets while maintaining design quality.

The methods generally fall into two broad categories: those used within the office during the design and contract document stage and those employed with contractors and materials suppliers.

Office procedures rely on a modular system and the construction of models as design tools. The modular system is based on a 3-foot, 4-inch (102-cm) plan unit and a stock material vertical unit. Models are made of balsa wood, which is usually recut and reglued as intersections and openings are studied. This approach builds on the modular system, which permits design complexities to be easily understood. Drawings are orderly but crowded with information in order to simplify communication with builders. More important is the client's participation in both programming and design; this makes the client conscious of his/her responsibilities for the success of the project.

Increasingly on newer projects, the owner has taken on a role as contractor, while relying on the architect as advisor. The owner is the contractor in the sense that multiple contracts are signed or agreed upon, after which De Vido coordinates their work on the owner's behalf. In its simplest form, this can be nothing more than a conventionally bid job with specialty procurement items such as cabinetwork, lighting fixtures, hardware, and furniture pulled out and bid separately.

In a more complex project, all mechanical trades (heating and air conditioning, electrical wiring, and plumbing), painting, flooring and floor finishing, tilework, and other similar trades are combined with the procurement items of the simpler approach, leaving only structural and other assembly work to a general contractor.

By combining office and field procedures, Alfredo De Vido is evolving a more precise way of building in which the architect has more control over quality and budget.

Boutique fits into landmarked building

Project: *Troa Cho, boutique, New York,
New York*
Architects: *Alfredo De Vido Associates,
Architects*
Project Manager: *David Cook*
Date Completed: *1982*

When a dress designer purchased a
landmarked building in New York's Upper
East Side Historic District, she planned
to open a shop on the ground floor in a
1650-square-foot (153-square-meter)
area. Three difficulties were immediately
apparent to the architects. First: How to
gain visibility from Madison Avenue to
the side street location? Second: How to
meet the deadline for opening the store in
time to show a fall line of fashions?
(Failure to meet the deadline could result
in the loss of thousands of dollars in
potential sales.) Third: How to procure
the New York City Landmarks Commission's approval within the time constraints?

The visibility and landmarks issues
were solved simultaneously by designing
a columnar feature separating the entrance door from the window and turning
it into a display case. Since the Landmarks' stipulations did not permit the
removal of the central masonry pier, this
device bridged the gap between door and
window and provided a unified display
area. A sculptural logo was placed on it to
catch the eyes of passersby on the
avenue.

The time deadline was met by award-
ing multiple contracts on the owner's
behalf. Some contracts, such as demolition, were awarded prior to the completion of documents to save time and reveal
hidden problems behind existing walls.

DESIGN FEATURES

Time constraints were the primary reason for doing this project on a design/
manage basis. Secondary reasons included the difficulties normally encountered in renovating an existing old
building and the unusual shapes of the
display cases, which required coordination between the cabinetmaker and electrician.

*Left: The landmarked
building required a sym-
pathetic solution for the
Troa Cho shop.*

*Below: The narrowness
of the existing space
called for a solution that
was open.*

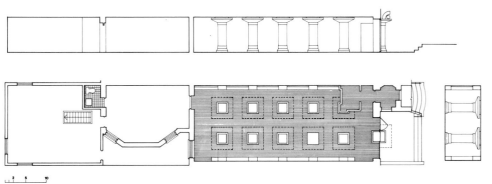

DESIGN/MANAGE TECHNIQUES

The architect recommended contractors to the owner, who signed multiple contracts and left the instruction and coordination of the various trades to the architect. The project manager was the same person who completed the construction documents. He had to spend one to two hours per day on site or in the office managing the project. The principal visited the project twice a week.

The design control remained with the architect, who made periodic recommendations to the owner for modifications or improvements to the originally approved drawings. The architect's position as project manager enabled them to make timely recommendations for design changes. For example, a change in the color mix of interior fluorescents was needed, as was the addition of tile to a badly cracked forecourt.

The architect agreed beforehand to bill the client on a time basis for all time spent during the construction phase of the work. Time billed for this purpose was in addition to a previously agreed-upon fixed fee for design services. Management time came to 8 percent of the final construction cost—far less than the customary 20 percent overhead and profit markup of general contractors.

COST CONTROL

The original estimate for the job was $100,000. Final costs were close to $135,000 for the following reasons:

1. Existing mechanical systems were in poor condition. Plumbing required extensive replacement not only to service the store, but also to safeguard it from water damage from a beauty salon above.

2. A serious structural defect was discovered after demolition was completed, requiring replacement of beams and support of the floor from the cellar below.

3. The owner upgraded the project during construction, adding mirrors, tiling the bathroom, finishing behind-the-scenes work areas, and making additional improvements.

The first two reasons were a result of unforeseen conditions common to renovation jobs. Note that alterations to the original design are easier to accomplish in a multiple contract arrangement. However, an owner should be aware that these changes will lead to higher overall costs.

SCHEDULE

The owner's deadline for completion of construction was met. On a normal architectural services/bid/general construction basis, this could not have been done, since bid periods require two to four weeks after completion of drawings. However, in this case, portions of the work were awarded prior to the completion of drawings: demolition was one; structural work was another.

Above: Display units were adapted for use as control desks and writing areas.

Top: Display fixtures within recall the exterior column and provide special areas.

Woman builds own house with architect's assistance

Project: *Cohalan house, Bayport, New York*
Architects: *Alfredo De Vido Associates, Architects*
Carpentry Foreman: *Frank Fussa*
Date Completed: *1983*

When the client, Mary Lou Cohalan, outlined her building program to Alfredo De Vido, she pointed out that she was familiar with construction techniques as a result of rebuilding her newspaper offices that had been destroyed by fire. With this experience behind her, Cohalan indicated that she would like to contract for many portions of the work on her house. She didn't know how to handle the structural aspects of the job, and De Vido suggested she employ a crew of carpenters under his supervision, which she did. The coordination of subcontractors was done by her, with advice from De Vido. The job progressed smoothly, and the results pleased both client and architect. Time was not a critical factor in this project.

The program called for three bedrooms—two small bedrooms for teenage children and a large master bedroom. A high water table ruled out the possibilities of a basement, and height restrictions ruled out a three-story house. A bermed lower level satisfied local zoning ordi-

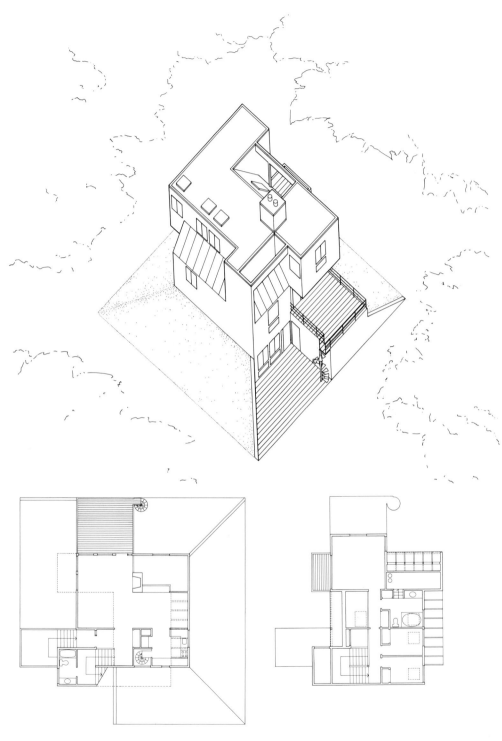

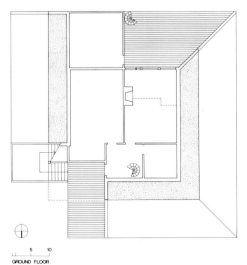

GROUND FLOOR

5 10

FIRST FLOOR

SECOND FLOOR

The plan is square, with protrusions and indentations. The main living spaces are on the first floor, with bedrooms on the second. The ground floor is partially below grade to conform with local codes.

nances, permitting some of these rooms to open out to the landscape. The raised main floor housed the living and dining areas, with a skylight open to the lowest level to allow more light to penetrate. The densely wooded site presented a light problem in general, so the design makes use of skylights in several areas to create bright interiors.

DESIGN FEATURES

The primary reason for using a design/manage approach on this job was Cohalan's desire to save money by using her connections with subcontractors and building materials suppliers. De Vido was also well acquainted with subcontractors in this area by virtue of his experience building houses as a general contractor. He was able to fill in any gaps in her knowledge.

DESIGN/MANAGE TECHNIQUES

De Vido designed the project in a normal way. Under construction, Cohalan engaged subcontractors known to her or solicited multiple bids from subcontractors of her own choosing or from those recommended by the architect. The carpentry crew did all the framing, sheathing, window installations, insulation, and much of the finishing. It was paid on a per diem basis. The carpentry foreman handled materials takeoffs, which were transmitted to the architect, who in turn ordered most of the materials for the owner.

The house was built as designed except for minor changes during construction. Such changes of finish or cabinets reflected Cohalan's growing understanding of the complex design. They were made in consultation with De Vido and were

generally upgradings of the originally specified quality levels. The framing and design finishes were executed by the carpentry crew under the direct supervision of the architect, thus avoiding any interpretation problems posed by the drawings. Material and equipment selections were routinely discussed by owner and architect and were made on the basis of preference, appearance, and durability, subject to overall cost control.

De Vido visited the site on an "as-needed" basis during the construction period. Due to Cohalan's experience with construction procedures and De Vido's previous work with the carpentry crew, a minimum of time was required.

The high water table required careful siting of the septic system. A problem developed in the installation of the skylights, which leached dirty residue onto

The cubical massing of the Cohalan house and free placement of the windows and doors were made understandable through the architect's use of a modular system.

Architect doubles as builder on built-for-sale house

Project: *Spechouse 6, East Hampton, New York*
Architects: *Alfredo De Vido Associates, Architects*
Date Completed: *1983*

Alfredo De Vido has regularly designed and constructed built-for-sale houses in a subdivision on eastern Long Island under his control. The program included approximately 3000 square feet (279 square meters) of space on 2 acres (.8 hectares) of land with three to four bedrooms, substantial living areas, luxurious baths, a pool, and integration of the architecture with the heritage of the community. The use of materials indigenous to and compatible with the environment in East Hampton was important, due to the intensity of the weather there. In addition, attention to fine detail is characteristic of the luxurious image that these weekend/vacation houses must project in order to sell. Subject to these constraints, De Vido sought to design a house that was economical to build.

DESIGN FEATURES

The dual goals of a well-designed house and a profitable project dictated evaluation at every stage. De Vido sought to combine easy-to-build forms in an architecturally interesting way and to carefully manage the process of building.

Plans of Spechouse 6 indicate a linear gable roof with shed add-on.

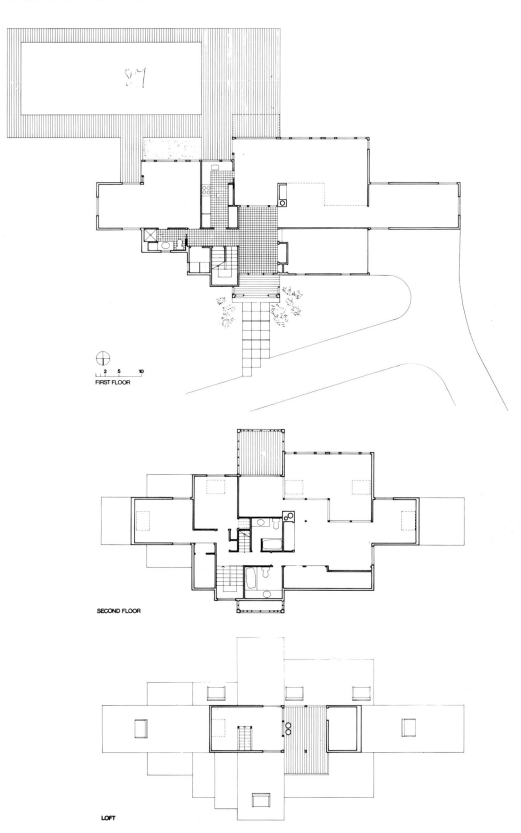

FIRST FLOOR

2 5 10

SECOND FLOOR

LOFT

DESIGN/MANAGE TECHNIQUES

Combining the roles of architect, contractor, and developer should have made things simple; however, the architect's design goals are not always compatible with the contractor's goal of ease of construction and the developer's goal of maximum profitability. For example, when the "architect" designed a large number of windows, the "contractor" weighed the amount of labor needed to install them, and the "developer" considered their cost. They passed this review because they enhanced the design of the house, thereby increasing its marketability.

Drawings consisted of ¼-inch (.6-cm) plans and sections, ⅛-inch (.3-cm) elevations, and a typical wall section. These were the minimum required to get a building permit.

The design, featuring a large gable 80 feet (24 meters) long and 10 feet (3 meters) wide with shed shapes resting against it, required careful alignment of roof slopes and junctures with the gable. The drawing noted all these meeting points. However, the brevity of the drawings assumed the continued on-site presence of the architect/manager to ensure that the design intent was carried through.

The design and drawings were done in De Vido's office. All contract negotiations and site direction were done by the architect/manager. Bid solicitation, materials ordering, and contract negotiations were done from the office by mail and telephone.

No contractor, manager, or architectural fee was paid during the course of the work. However, whenever the house is sold, a substantial profit will be distributed to the architect/manager.

COST CONTROL

The original goal was to hold actual costs within $115,000. This total did not include land or architect/manager/contractor fees. Actual costs came to $125,000, due to the addition of a driveway and various upgradings of materials and design features during the progress of the work. This points up one of the problems inherent in a design/build situation. It is easy to upgrade the design or the materials along the way since there is no lump sum price that must be agreed to by a third party.

Carpenters were paid individually at the completion of work each Saturday by De Vido, who used a special contractor account. Other subcontractors were paid upon completion of various phases of their work. Since no financing was necessary, it was possible to organize the work without regard to normal bank payment schedules. These schedules often provide for the payment of certain trades, such as plumbing and heating, at the end of the job. However, it is easier to get these trades to meet contractor's schedules if they know they will get paid promptly.

SCHEDULE

Time was of the essence, since it appeared that mortgage money for potential buyers was available and comparatively cheap at the time construction began. Due to De Vido's commitment to office work in New York, all the critical carpentry phases took place on Friday or Saturday, when the carpentry crew and architect/manager were both available.

The work took place from May to October 1983 and proceeded as follows:
Week 1:
Excavation: Clearing and excavation.

Week 2:
Masonry: Foundation completed.

Week 3:
Carpentry: Floor beams and supporting posts and ½-inch (1.3-cm) plywood subfloor completed. First floor partitions laid out.

Week 4:
Carpentry: Floor partitions and half of the second floor beams erected, complete with subfloor.

Week 5:
Carpentry: Second floor partitions and part of roof erected.

Week 6:
Carpentry: Roof framing completed. Exterior sheathing of the stud construction begun.
Electrical: A bid solicited three weeks previously from a well-recommended bidder looked high, so another was solicited.
Plumbing: A satisfactory price had been solicited three weeks previously from a plumber who had worked with the architect on three houses prior to this. He

was alerted that he could begin work in two to three weeks.
Heating: The heating contractor required steady prodding to submit his estimate. Since the architect had worked previously on five houses with the contractor, he knew the contractor required pushing.
Septic: Septic installation was started and aborted four hours later, due to excessive ground water caused by a rainy spring. It was agreed that work would be resumed in August when the ground was expected to be drier.

Week 7:
Carpentry: Exterior sheathing of walls with ½-inch (1.3-cm) plywood completed and exterior windows set.
Roofing: Roof shingler clad half the roof with asphalt shingles and set three of six roof windows. Bids were solicited from hot roofers since three small areas required such skills.
Prefab fireplace/chimney: Scheduled a week before, work was completed in a day.

Week 8:
Carpentry: Installation of exterior windows and doors completed and exterior siding begun. Some "blocking" on inside begun. (Blocking is a time-consuming chore that takes place upon completion of the floor joists, interior partitions, and roof beams. It consists of bracing the beams and rafters at half or third points, filling in around windows and doors so the finishes will meet those units properly, and constructing closet rough framing and cabinet supports. This is an important phase of the work that must be supervised closely for architectural reasons.) It required several days of architect/manager's time to get it right.
Roofing: Roof shingler completed work, including installation of remaining roof windows.
Hot roofing: After some difficulty contacting a qualified subcontractor to do hot roofing (flat roofs), architect/manager instructed a responding bidder to proceed with the work on a time-and-material basis, since it seemed too difficult to get bids in a timely way and lack of a watertight roof would slow most other work in the house.
Electrical: Second bidder was 40 percent lower than first; he was advised to schedule the work.

Well: Well driller was contacted, but busy. However, in view of his work on other houses, he agreed to schedule work within the next few weeks.

Sheetrock and insulation: These two subcontracts can be done by separate firms. Firm selected had done satisfactory work on previous houses, so a bid was solicited. Since it was within budget projections, firm was advised to schedule work within two weeks.

Heating/Air conditioning: With bid forthcoming, subcontractor advised to schedule work as soon as possible. (Subcontractors in mechanical and electrical trades sometimes procrastinate until advised that they must do work or else trades to follow will be held up. If convinced this is so, work usually gets done in time. If it doesn't, subcontractor is poorly organized, and another should be sought for next job.)

Plumbing: Plumber cut holes and commenced roughing. Plumbing and heating subcontractors showed up on the same day, a help in coordinating routes of their pipes and ducts. These two subs can sometimes be in conflict, since their specialties frequently follow the same routes to the basement/crawl space/utility room where they originate and return.

Top: Shed extensions abut the long gable roof on the back of Spechouse 6 and provide additional interior space as required. The 80-foot (24-meter) gable unifies the composition.

Above: A grid pattern of cedar two by fours is the predominant design motif of Spechouse 6. Note how it is repeated on the second and third floor terraces on the front of the house.

Stock windows grouped to form a patterned wall produce constantly changing lighting effects on the interior.

Week 9:

Carpentry: Installation of siding and blocking continued. Town inspection of framing requested.

Patio doors: Separate subcontractor called in to install two sliding patio doors. This proved to be a good idea, since work went quickly and was economical. (Carpenters can install patio doors, but this particular crew does not enjoy the work.)

Hot roofing: Subcontractor started work one day and completed it the following. (This specialty is messy, and should be scheduled before finishes are installed.)

Heating/Air conditioning: Ductwork was installed in those areas above crawl space that were to be sheetrocked. Furnace

delivered and placed in crawl space, since it is easier to do before walls and floors are finished.

Stairs: Drawings were forwarded to the stair builder, bid approved, and delivery of stairs scheduled for following week.

Interior doors/trim: Measurements taken for the sizes and amounts of interior doors and trim, and an order placed with supplier for delivery within two weeks.

Plumbing: Roughing completed, and town inspector scheduled for water test. This inspection was combined with a framing inspection.

Electrical: Wiring within walls begun after consultation with architect/manager.

Week 10:

Carpentry: Installation of siding completed, decks on second floor and loft terraces completed, and stairs installed.

Town inspection: Town inspector approved water test for plumbing and, after requesting some additional bracing, approved the framing.

Sheetrock/Insulation: House fully insulated.

Electrical: Electrical roughing completed.

Heating/Air conditioning: Roughing completed.

Week 11:

Carpentry: Exterior wood trim completed. Installation of wood flooring begun.

Sheetrock/Insulation: Sheetrock installed throughout.

Week 12:

Carpentry: Installation of wood flooring continued.

Interior doors and trim: Doors and trim ordered.

Sheetrock/insulation: First coat of spackle installed.

Week 13:

Carpentry: No work this week to complete spackling of sheetrock.

Sheetrock/insulation: Second coat of spackle completed.

Week 14:

Carpentry: Wood flooring completed. Installation of interior doors, trim, and shelving begun.

Sheetrock/insulation: Third (final) coat of spackle and sanding begun in preparation for painting.

Week 15:

Carpentry: Work on trim, interior and exterior, started.

Painting: Several prices solicited; painters visited job to estimate work. (Note that painting prices are best solicited when sheetrock and trim are completely in place. Painters are not practiced in estimating from drawings. This can work to the contractor's advantage or disadvantage, since it is possible for a painter to underestimate a job with high ceilings or an unusual design feature. It is also possible for him to overestimate the work in an effort to compensate for inability to read drawings. However, it is not good to have a subcontractor on the job who is doing the work at a low profit margin or at a loss. He will try to cut corners or use inferior materials.)

Heating/air conditioning: Contractor began installing ductwork in crawl space. This represents much of his work. (It is not work of an urgent nature, since other work can proceed without holding this up.)

Pool: Installer started digging hole for pool.

Well: Well and pump installed.

Week 16:

Carpentry: Trim essentially completed and ready for painting.

Tile: Tile subcontractor scheduled for following week. No estimate was necessary since he had given a square-foot price for each of the different types of tile, and it was easy to figure the bill at completion of work.

Painter: Work begun.

Pool: Work on excavation and installation of steel side walls, piping, and plastic liner continued.

Septic: Ground sufficiently dry to permit installation of septic system.

Week 17:

Carpentry: With pool walls completed, carpenters could begin installation of decking.

Painter: Work continues.

Tile: Work completed.

Cabinetry: Cabinetmaker, who worked on architect's previous houses as a subcontractor, alerted that work was ready for field measurement.

Week 18:

Carpentry: Deck completed.

Excavation subcontractor: Since pool excavation was completed and pool installer had been directed where to pile excess fill, excavator could backfill and finish grade around house.

Painter: Work completed. (Despite the fact that painter had done other jobs satisfactorily for architect, this particular one turned out fairly sloppy.) Painter requested to return in next weeks for touch-ups.

Week 19:

Cabinetry: Installation of cabinets begun.

Electrician: Returned to job to begin installation of fixtures and device plates.

Pool: Completed.

The second story handrails and screens were designed during construction.

Week 20:

Cabinetry: Cabinet installation completed.

Electrician: Fixture installation completed.

Week 24–26: Remainder of construction period spent coordinating final phases of subcontractors' work, listing incomplete or below-standard work, and organizing such landscape items as driveway, paths, and planting/seeding.

Scheduling of this work showed that it could be done in a reasonably efficient and profitable way if the architect/manager was willing and able to set aside approximately 10 to 15 hours a week for this project. Much of the work did not conflict with architectural work during normal office hours, since most coordination had to be done on the phone between 7 and 8 A.M. or in the early evening. On-site coordination in this case was done on Saturdays or an occasional Friday, but such off-hour work presumes that the architect/manager is willing to work long days and weeks.

In most cases, things worked out well when the subcontractor selected had worked for the architect/manager previously and knew his quality and schedule demands. In addition, a reliable odd-job man was hired to do the innumerable small tasks needed at the end of construction.

Owner builds underground house

Project: *Moore house, Sharon, Connecticut*
Architects: *Alfredo De Vido Associates*
                Structural engineer: Paul Gossen
Project Associate: *David Cook*
Date Completed: *1984*

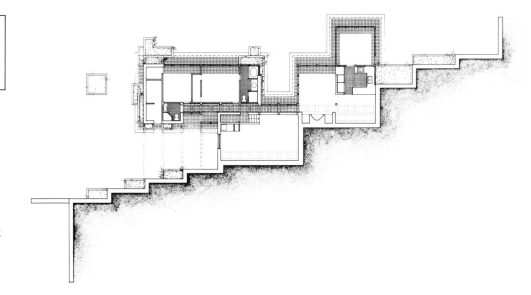

The program for this house was unusual in that:

1. It was to be built underground.

2. Materials included oak posts and beams cut from trees on the site and stone blasted during excavation work for the house's foundations.

3. The owner, although inexperienced at contracting, wanted to build his own house.

4. The owner was a graphic artist with high design and quality standards.

All these factors were discussed by Richard Moore and Alfredo De Vido before work was begun. Since they had worked together before, such an approach to the project made sense. A budget was drawn up to cover a two-bedroom, two-bath house, with living room, kitchen, dining room and studio. A screened porch was to be included off the kitchen and living room.

DESIGN FEATURES

The house is an earth-sheltered construction, with deep overhangs covering south-facing glass to provide shading from summer sun; stone-faced concrete walls to retain earth and define entry on the north side; structural members to be sized by the engineer and cut from on-site oaks; stone and tile floors on concrete slabs to promote thermal mass for solar gain in the winter; warm air circulatory system to provide heat from central furnace to slab; drainable plumb-

Above: Final plans proved helpful to owner Richard Moore when working with craftsmen and contractors during the construction of his home, which he supervised.

Right: This view across the pond to the Moore house shows its earth-covered roof blending with the crest of the hill.

ing to accommodate times in the winter when the house is not in use; a landscape scheme to prevent untidy roof growth; and wiring, piping, and ducting to be concealed within the exposed structure.

DESIGN/MANAGE TECHNIQUES

After De Vido visited the site and outlined a program, he came up with preliminary drawings, the second scheme of which was accepted by Moore.

The final drawings took three months and were more complete than normally required for a house. The fact that it was underground was an important factor. Details needed careful investigation and the various options for the selection of techniques required review. Loads are unusually high in earth-sheltered construction, and the advice of the structural engineer was sought frequently.

Based on initial budgets and advice from De Vido about dividing the job into various contracts, Moore interviewed local craftsmen and selected them as the job progressed or as various trades were required. This approach is desirable in earth-covered construction on a rocky site, since subcontractors such as masons and excavators do not know what site problems exist below the ground surface and they cannot forecast accurately what their labor costs will be. Moore negotiated with the subcontractors, employing them with different arrangements—some on a per diem or hourly basis and others on a lump sum where the scope of work was clear enough to permit this. (See pages 84–85 for Moore's comments.)

Due to the completeness of the drawings, Moore consulted with De Vido mostly by telephone. He needed advice about changes of detail or technique proposed by the craftsmen working on the house.

It is not unusual in the building industry to have a number of technical options available to achieve a desired end result. Some of these involve design decisions, but most are concerned with weatherproofing possibilities or the proper sequencing of operations. In earth-sheltered construction, for instance, there are four or five different ways of waterproofing the roof. Proper waterproofing is essential, since failure to do so will require the removal of tons of earth to find a leak.

Dimensional coordination among owner, architect, and builder was important, since procurement of additional timber from the site was difficult and required months of drying time.

Stones for the walls were excavated from the site. The owner interviewed several masons and reviewed their work before selecting one.

Although De Vido and Moore researched these options carefully, their selection of a material and installation sequence was questioned periodically by subcontractors. It is important not to ignore such questions, since the success or failure of any detail ultimately rests with the person doing on-site work. Therefore some suggestions were politely turned aside; others were incorporated as positive improvements at little or no change in contract price. A number of questions concerned structural sizes and connections. The structural engineer, a well-qualified person with whom De Vido had a long professional relationship, as a rule refused requests to alter these details in any major way, citing the big loads common to earth-covered construction. In such situations it is essential to follow the recommendations of the engineer.

Some materials, such as the skylight, were procured separately by the owner through the architect, since it was possible to get a larger discount that way. The approach makes sense where the savings are significant. However, it is not generally recommended for such items as plumbing fixtures: Assuming the plumber is not marking up his routinely discounted price excessively, it is better to let him procure such items. They will at times arrive from the factory with defects, in which case it is the plumber's responsibility to send them back or have them repaired. If the owner has done the purchasing, responsibility to remedy the defect is also his.

Most of the workers were local. The roof membrane, a substance called "Bentonite," required special installation techniques not commonly used by roofing contractors. De Vido solicited the names of several contractors recommended by the company, and a qualified installer was brought in from Pittsburgh to do the work.

COST CONTROL

Costs are within original projections.

SCHEDULE

Construction extended over a three-year period.

Comments by Richard Moore on Taking over as Architect/Contractor

Over a five-year period my wife, Noriko, and I carved out a 1-acre (.4-hectares) pond and built a private campground on 23 acres (9 hectares) of remote wooded land in northwest Connecticut. As we steadily thinned the trees around the pond during the changing seasons and more of the rolling terrain revealed itself, I imagined that I would design a house that would look like it grew out of the land, even using some of the materials found on it for the construction.

Could I do it alone? Why not. After all, I had designed exhibits larger than the house I had in mind. After completing preliminary plan and elevation drawings over an Independence Day weekend, I came to my senses and realized that I had just enough knowledge to be dangerous. To resolve even the technical problems of the house that was shaping up I would need professional help.

Fortunately, I had worked with architect Al De Vido on a house demonstrating energy conservation principles for a public utility the previous year. I knew him to be very knowledgeable about his profession, we shared common esthetic interests, and I thought that he might permit a collaborative effort in which the owner could become far more involved in the design process than usual. I was delighted when he accepted my offer.

The site I had selected, the earth-sheltered profile, the use of oak timbers cut from my land, and other plans of mine were retained, but the collaboration soon resulted in a much more interesting organization of space. By Labor Day the preliminary plans were done. By Christmas a notch had been blasted out of a knoll overlooking the pond. By New Year's Day, some 90 oak trees had been felled, soon to be milled into posts, beams, and lintels, and then stacked to dry in the open air of a local saw mill.

The plans underwent steady refinement over the winter and construction began in the spring. Wearing the hats of architect, general contractor, and optimist, I had to represent the plans to the subcontractors I selected.

From the experiences of a friend who had built a house nearby, my own campsite contracting, and some sleuthing, I had a good idea of who were the best subcontractors in the area. Only four of them were asked to bid on a flat price basis—the blasting contractor, excavator, concrete mason, and the Bentonite waterproofing contractor.

Because of the unusual construction of the house, I felt that the other subcontractors would build too much of a cushion into a flat price bid. The plumbing/heating contractor worked on a time-and-materials basis with a cost ceiling. The stone mason worked on a price per square foot basis for labor plus materials. All other subcontractors worked on a simple time-and-materials basis.

Being both the contractor and the on-site "architect" required a surprising amount of my time. I managed to be on site at least one working day per week. A full week was spent with the various trades to position the electrical, plumbing, and heating before the slab floor was poured. Several times each week telephone conversations were required to coordinate the trades and resolve questions. For questions over my head, I sought advice from De Vido.

Any remorse I felt for not trying to do some of the finished drawings myself was soon forgotten as I found myself drafting a steady flow of small drawings to resolve details. One of this century's most respected architects has said that "God is in the details." While this is certainly true, he failed to mention that the devil is in them as well. Architecture is a process, not a set of plans. The homeowner who takes on the role of architect after the plans are in hand should be prepared to spend more time than the architect would in implementing them.

The house is now 90 percent closed in, and the soil roof was planted with ground cover this spring. Much remains to be done (those details again), but the end is in sight.

I think the house will be a success. This week the stonemason's helper wrote us to say that he hopes we will continue with the exterior stonework when warm weather comes. It seems that he kind of likes the place. So do we.

All beams and posts were cut from on-site oaks and stacked for drying prior to use. The precise relationship of the structural members was discussed and coordinated between owner and architect.

Phased renovation meets space needs of growing firm

Project: *Offices for Muir Cornelius Moore, Inc., New York, New York*
Architects: *Alfredo De Vido Associates, Architects*
Date Completed: *1983*

Over a period of six months, the graphics firm of Muir Cornelius Moore (MCM) expanded their business into several new areas. Knowing that their space needs would be significantly greater, they reviewed alternative office spaces outside the building in which they were located. But after due consideration they decided to stay put.

Their office building has an elevator system that divides stops into groups of floors, and the firm decided to lease new space within one group of floors, so that employees might have easier access to one another. Alfredo De Vido phased the renovations as the various spaces became available.

DESIGN FEATURES

Primary design emphasis was placed in the reception area and conference room, since these spaces convey the firm's design image. Richard Moore, the Creative Director, had designed a modular system of furniture, already in use when the new space was renovated and wanted to continue using this line. De Vido then fit the office furniture system into newly acquired spaces after subdividing them as efficiently as possible. Other than in special use areas, building standard was used for ceiling, floor, and lighting treatments within offices and corridors.

Above: The entrance lobby of Muir Cornelius Moore, Inc., features a pattern of small squares in the carpet and back wall. Plants are changed seasonally.

Right: A lighting consultant was retained to provide even illumination on the recessed wall squares, which have different colors on each side.

DESIGN/MANAGE TECHNIQUES

The overall job was broken into six phases related to the times when space was vacated by other firms on the floor. De Vido worked with Moore in planning the space and working out details.

The initial phase was awarded to the low bidder of a selected contractor's list. Although he enjoyed a competitive advantage by being on the job, bids were solicited on later phases as well. Air conditioning, carpet, and cabinetwork were all separately procured. A lighting consultant was called in for the reception areas, since the lighting of the recessed pattern of squares behind the receptionist was important.

COST CONTROL

Much of the work was to the particular building's standard and was paid for by the building as part of the leasing arrangement. Special construction and consultants' time was also billed to and paid for by the owner.

SCHEDULE

The job was done on a fast-track basis, since the space was urgently needed. Progress was generally satisfactory.

Above: This media wall fits within the design idiom of the firm's modular furniture system.

Left: Adjustable lighting and a variety of display and media systems were important in the conference room.

New house in landmarks district blends with 19th-century neighbors

Project: *222 Columbia Heights, Brooklyn, New York*
Owner: *Ian Bruce Eichner*
Architects: *Alfredo De Vido Associates, Architects*
Construction Manager: *Saul Gersen*
Date Completed: *1980*

Brooklyn Heights, a Landmarks Preservation District within New York City, is noted for its four-story brownstone houses, many of which were completed in the late 19th century in the Renaissance Revival style. Blending a contemporary house with older neighbors in this community at first posed a problem.

Ian Bruce Eichner's original program was for a two- to three-story house to be built on a vacant piece of land at the end of a row of handsome brownstones. But talks with the Landmarks Preservation Commission led to a revision in this program, the effect of which was to make the height of the building equal to that of the adjacent structures. The house now contains a triplex unit [3,800 square feet (353 square meters)], two condominium units [1320 and 670 square feet (123 and 62 square meters) respectively], and a rental unit [570 square feet (53 square meters)].

Below: The scale and details of the new structure recall the row of existing 19th-century Renaissance Revival buildings in Brooklyn Heights. Note that in areas where windows were not desirable, blank recesses were provided with sill and headpieces similar to those of the windows.

Right: Room layouts, which vary from floor to floor, were centered on the window locations: top, triplex floor; middle, condominium; bottom, rental unit.

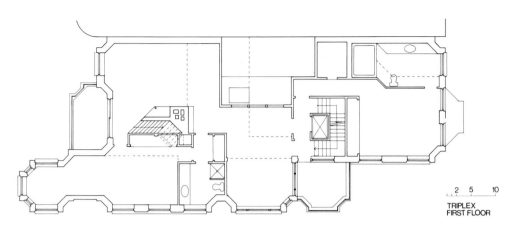

TRIPLEX
FIRST FLOOR

2 5 10

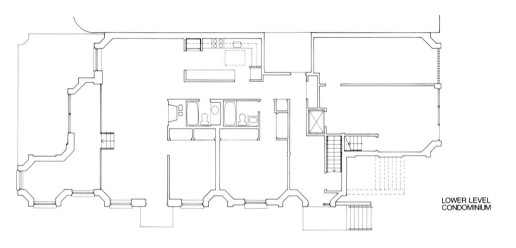

LOWER LEVEL
CONDOMINIUM

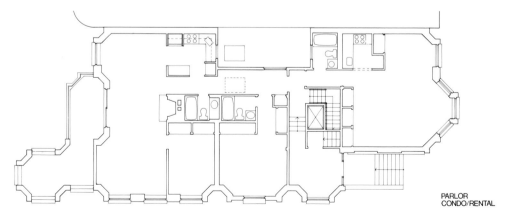

PARLOR
CONDO/RENTAL

DESIGN FEATURES

Alfredo De Vido's design respects the character of the surrounding buildings. These houses are made of closed masonry walls, punctured regularly with windows that are large at the parlor floor and become smaller in the upper stories. They often have an unusual entrance feature or bay window and a picturesque skyline.

The new building provides the same arrangement of openings, enlivened by cornices and belt courses. Within, spaces are contemporary in shape, thereby increasing the apparent size of the rooms. Generous window areas bring natural light to all parts of the house while offering a splendid view of lower Manhattan.

DESIGN/MANAGE TECHNIQUES

Since this building was erected for a developer who employed a full-time construction manager, the design and construction segments of the work proceeded in tandem during some periods.

After an initial program had been worked out, preliminary design was a matter of working with the New York City Landmarks Commission, whose approval was a necessary first step toward gaining a building permit. The main issue concerned the kind of new construction that is compatible with the old buildings in the Landmarks District. Was it to be construction that reproduced the style and details of the existing buildings or construction that harmonized current design elements with the old buildings?

Both owner and architect wanted to build a contemporary building. However, there was an active and articulate group of neighbors who believed that only a 19th-century style was appropriate, and a public debate ensued at the commission's hearings about what style was harmonious.

The Landmarks Commission rejected the first two designs as inappropriate, since they were smaller in scale and differed in character from the neighboring row of buildings. But after conversations among the owner, local groups, and several members of the Landmarks Commission, a third design was presented that increased the bulk of the building to match that of its neighbors. Also a different window pattern was designed, using the idiom of the 19th-century row houses.

Although this design was accepted, De Vido asked the owner/developer if he could present a fourth scheme to the commission, refining details and incorporating a system of moldings and belt courses to reflect the richness of detail in the older structures. Approval was given for this final step and the building was built to this design. Construction management was handled by Saul Gersen, who worked out many details in the field, while consulting with De Vido on sensitive design issues.

COST CONTROL

Original budget projections were based on a smaller building with a loosely defined program, so final costs were considerably higher. The construction manager monitored costs under construction and consulted regularly with the owner and architect to select materials and techniques that would produce the desired esthetic and technical results at reasonable cost.

SCHEDULE

The schedule had to be extended because the owner-developer had a fire disaster on another project.

Above: Although the window pattern was set by the dictates of the Landmarks Preservation Commission, it was possible to use a freer spatial concept within the triplex.

Left: Sill and head pieces for the windows were precast in concrete in a color to match the brick.

Left: A cozy seating alcove frames a view of lower Manhattan.

Below: Interior walls and geometries reflect the identation of the exterior.

TADAO ANDO ARCHITECT & ASSOCIATES
Osaka, Japan

Construction-oriented architect limits his palette of materials

The practice of Tadao Ando differs from that of many other Japanese architectural firms in two important aspects: first, its regional character is based on the traditions of the city of Osaka; second, it takes an artisanlike approach to construction.

Because Tokyo is the dominant city in Japan, most Japanese architects find their practices revolve around it. However, it is a source of pride to Ando that his office and most of his work are in the city of Osaka. The traditions of that city have been based on intimacy between people and nature, yet blight and pollution have damaged this relationship over the years. Ando has addressed this conflict between cultural heritage and physical reality in his architecture. His solution is to design houses with facades closed to the street and yet open within, often centered around garden courts or semienclosed outdoor spaces.

Ando limits his palette of materials to reinforced concrete and glass. Due to his attraction for work of skilled artisans, he keeps a close eye on the technical aspects of each job, particularly the making of concrete. What results is particularly fine workmanship.

Ando notes that drawings are the means that resolve the desires and requirements of client, builder, site, and architect. Axonometrics, sketches, plans, and sections are used intensively in the design stage, after which working drawings are produced. In Japan, working drawings convey the design intent to the contractor, who then produces an extensive set of shop drawings. Construction is based on these after approval by the architect. This approach is quite common with bigger buildings in the United States and Europe, but unusual with houses.

In Ando's case, the concrete drawings are the most important ones, since this material is the main one used. Jointing, form, tie locations, and pour separation lines are scrutinized carefully after submittal by the contractor to the architect. Since the use of reinforced concrete is well understood by Japanese contractors who use it extensively in this earthquake-prone country, it is not necessary to supervise the site work on a day-to-day basis once the design intent is established.

Given a new job, Ando initially seeks the key ingredient in his client's lifestyle. He recognizes the difficulty of incorporating all aspects of the client's needs and therefore singles out one or two important points to emphasize in the architectural composition. He believes that the client's lifestyle will inevitably change within the new spaces in the house and that through the stimulation of the environment self-discovery will be promoted.

Key ingredient in client's lifestyle chosen as basis for house design

Project: *Koshino house, Ashiya, Japan*
Architects: *Tadao Ando Architect & Associates*
Date Completed: *1981*

The essential factor in this commission was the combination of professional and domestic requirements of the owner, a fashion designer. She sought wide exterior steps, space to entertain in, and space in which to display her designs to small groups. The building was also planned to house a three-generation family—grandmother, parents, four children—as well as a maid.

Another major consideration was the site, located in a national park, where legal height and setback requirements had to be taken into account.

DESIGN FEATURES

The architect hoped to disturb the beautiful site as little as possible and initially envisaged a concrete box half buried in a hillside of greenery. However, the site sloped to the southeast away from the road, and the slope, combined with a limited building area, ruled out this possibility. A two-box solution was worked out, separated by a stepped semi-enclosed court. The two units were connected on the lower level by an enclosed subterranean corridor. The slope permitted the extensive glass areas to be oriented to the south which faced the view.

A large stepped court is used for the owner's fashion shows, with models posing on and below the steps. The adjacent corridor features a series of slit windows that are terminated at the steps outside, providing a lively visual impression within the corridor. The kitchen across the court has the same feature. Vantage points within are more varied than the simple exterior might lead one to expect. From the high-ceilinged living room, extensive glass looks out across the landscaped courtyard, past the wall of the bedroom wing, toward glimpses of the countryside beyond.

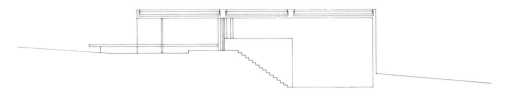

The grade difference is steep, as shown in this section of the Koshino residence.

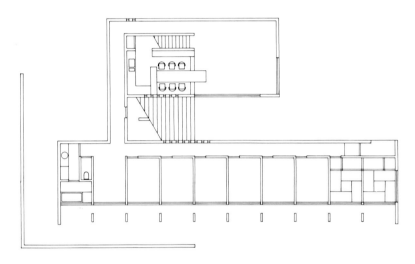

Bedrooms are lined up in a uniform row, with the living/dining areas in a separate wing.

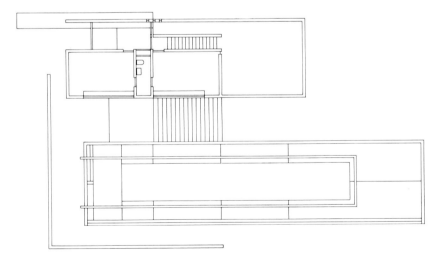

Upper levels reveal the entrance and void over the living room.

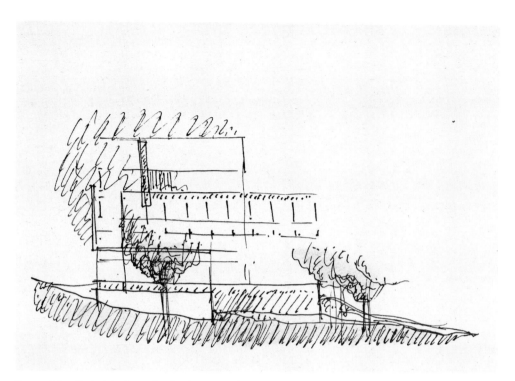

The architect's sketch shows the basic concept.

The roof of the bedroom wing is supported by a uniform row of concrete piers.

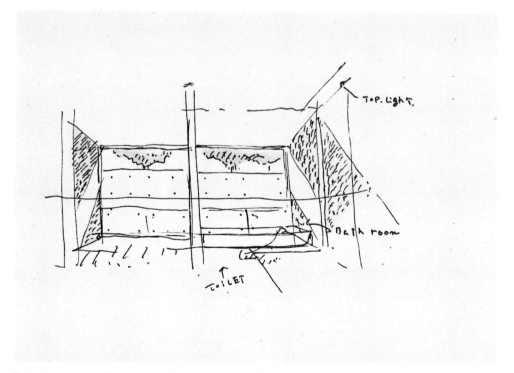

This interior sketch illustrates the living room area, with top light and a high view from the space.

Intriguing slits of light illuminate the bedroom wing corridor.

A dramatic shadow shows the exposed texture of the concrete.

Spatial experiences within are varied due to the stepping of the elements. From the entry, one goes down a full flight of stairs to the living room, in which light is introduced from above and toward the view. Adjacent to it is the compact kitchen/dining area; behind this, the subterranean corridor leads to the bedroom wing, where identical chambers are lined up in a row facing south.

DESIGN/MANAGE TECHNIQUES

In keeping with the architect's philosophy of extracting the key ingredient of the owner's lifestyle and apotheosizing it, the living room and stepped court are responsive to the owner's work and social needs. The extended family is expressed in the long row of bedrooms with a colonnade outside them.

Construction is limited to concrete and glass, built after the contractor's shop drawings had been approved by the architect. Due to the nature of the material, poured concrete is economical when composed in large flat walls. The design recognizes this, and windows are composed in broad expanses. Detail junctions of the windows to the concrete are restricted in number. This is also economical, since the builder did not have to deal with a great variety of different conditions. It also simplified the architect's job, since the chances for error were diminished once a detail had been successfully established.

COST CONTROL

Costs were within original projections.

SCHEDULE

There were no special schedule demands. The house was completed without notable schedule delays.

FEILDEN CLEGG DESIGN

The Architecture Shop
Partners: Richard Feilden, Peter Clegg
Bath, England

Architects' in-house building company expands client/ developer role

Some of Feilden Clegg Design's early work was carried out on a design/build basis with clients who trusted them sufficiently to contract for the work on a cost-plus arrangement with the general contractor. The success of these early projects led them to establish an in-house building company that proved to be a springboard to larger and more interesting building projects, some of which feature low-energy design and passive solar applications.

Feilden Clegg Design notes that traditional procedure in England is competitive bidding on specifications and drawings produced by the architect. For projects over $250,000, a quantity surveyor is hired to produce a "bill of quantities" that contractors then price. After the client employs the architect as an agent to advise on the contract between himself and the builder, the resultant relationship often causes problems, since it allows each party to blame the third party in his/her absence and leaves various roles undefined. This arrangement also leads to a very long precontract period, since the entire building must be designed before soliciting bids.

There has been a move toward management contracting in England for large building projects and increasingly for smaller ones. Management contractors—usually experienced contractors with national reputations—work for a flat fee of approximately 2 percent to serve the general contractor and organize all the subcontract work.

Feilden Clegg Design currently deals with contracts up to around $500,000 and has experimented with different ways to get things built. The firm's own building company is now used to provide a complete design-and-build service. The building company exists solely to carry out projects that come through the architectural office. It is currently developing expertise in development, management of larger projects, and new technologies. One result is that feedback to the architectural practice is of enormous benefit in achieving a better understanding of what details are required in the field.

Speculative housing designed for minimum energy use

Project: *Cleveland Reach, Bath, England*
Architects: *Feilden Clegg Design*
Date Completed: *1983*

This project is a group of eight speculative riverside apartments near the center of Bath that Feilden Clegg Design embarked on as part of its program to expand work by undertaking its own development. Although the architects lacked the necessary collateral for a large development project, their local bank manager was convinced to lend them the money because their application included input from realtors, estimators, and subcontractors. This also contained a summary of the project's cash-flow requirements over an 18-month period using a spreadsheet microcomputer program.

The project includes two types of apartments: single-level apartments on the ground floor [61 square meters (219 square feet)] and upper-floor duplexes [74 square meters (266 square feet)].

The architects feel that the development has proved that good design and energy conservation can sell within a stylistically traditional market. The apartments were designed to meet the double insulation values required by building regulations in the United Kingdom. Triple glazing was incorporated as a standard feature, and the two end units incorporate a ventilation system with heat recovery that cuts infiltration loss by about 60 percent. These two apartments also have experimental sections of "Trombe wall" (heat-retaining) masonry, so that the overall space heating load is reduced to an absolute minimum.

The development is completely sold. Feilden Clegg Design is planning further experimental development work, which now accounts for around 20 percent of their total workload. Experience in development and an understanding of the pressures that a developer operates under have enabled the practice to offer a broader range of services to clients, as well as enabling them to initiate projects and advise on development and financing at a very early stage.

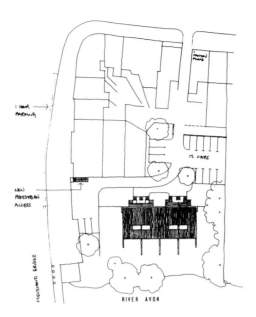

Left: The site plan for Cleveland Reach shows the relation of the building to the river view and the existing townscape.

Below: Line elevation drawings were used to explain the building to prospective buyers: below, street entrance; bottom, river side.

DESIGN FEATURES

Pitched tile roofs and a domestic-scale building were designed to fit within the traditional community of Bath. Innovative plans were developed to fit within the steep roofs. An open facade faced toward the river.

DESIGN/MANAGE TECHNIQUES

The client-developer role was allocated to one of the principals, Richard Feilden, who took it upon himself to make the project work financially. The firm therefore had the three basic roles of client, architect, and builder under one roof. Each person had equal responsibility to make sure that the project worked from his own viewpoint. Because it was the firm's first development project, the preparatory work took a long time. One scheme was eventually rejected by everyone, and under pressure from the "client," realtors were brought in for advice.

Most of the work was subcontracted after soliciting competitive bids. The only direct labor consisted of three carpenters and two laborers. The person fulfilling the contractor role during the design also carried through the work as the architect's project manager. A quantity sur-

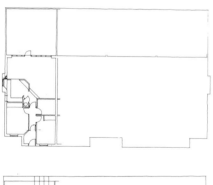

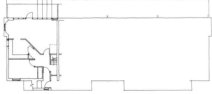

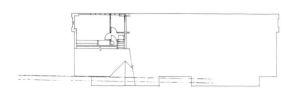

Left: Plans of the end units show entries to stacked units and grouping of entrances to upper units in pairs.

Above: These gable entrances have decorative lattice trim that gives each front door a sense of individuality.

Overall view shows the grouping of the eight entrances into two protruding gable ends.

veyor was employed for an initial cost analysis. His information was subsequently rewritten to suit the actual building process.

Because of the risks involved, the architect did not put much effort into schematic drawings for planning permission. These were free-hand sketches, colored to indicate different materials. A model was also produced that proved useful for preselling some of the units.

Changes requested by the tenants were carried out through discussions with the architect in subsequent negotiations. The architects lost money on most of this work and have learned that it must be carried out in a more organized fashion, with adequate allowance to cover disputes. In future work, they intend to offer a more specific range of alternatives.

Planning control and building regulations such as construction detailing, fire precautions, lighting, ventilation, and space standards were tightly controlled and permits were required. It was also necessary to get planning permission for this is a relatively unusual building in the center of Bath, where virtually every building is landmarked.

The construction company was paid all costs plus 12 percent to cover overhead. The architectural practice was paid fees based on the number of hours worked, which amounted to 9 percent.

COST CONTROL

The budget was allowed to float upward as the architects realized the units were underpriced. This led to a large difference in price between two comparable units—the first of which was sold at $47,000 in January 1982 and the other at $60,000 in October of the same year. This finally resulted in an overall profit of 15 percent plus all overheads and a small profit in the architectural fee. This is what they originally set out to make. They are in the process of streamlining cost control procedures.

Top: Windows are integrated with the solar wall, with awnings to provide sun control.

Right: Rear facade uses glass to catch the river view and provide for passive solar features.

SCHEDULE

To complete the first unit, a tight timetable was exceeded by one month. Construction started in September 1982, with the first unit completed in April 1983 and the final unit in November 1983. A reasonably mild winter helped the schedule. Prefabrication was also important. The windows are factory glazed (three layers of glass) and painted. This proved convenient and now the architects prefabricate wherever possible for improved quality and better scheduling. Precast concrete floors proved advantageous, since 250 square meters (897 square feet) in a day could be set in place.

JERSEY DEVIL

Steve Badanes, Jim Adamson, John Ringel, Greg Torchio
Stockton, New Jersey

Architects/builders move to individual sites to design/build

The provocative name of this firm derives from a character in New Jersey folklore who has been described as an impish, nattily dressed creature with batlike wings, cloven hoofs, horns, and a forked tail. He is reputed to delight in scaring people half out of their wits.

Steve Badanes, one of the principals of Jersey Devil, says that the firm tries to create a form strong enough to support individual creativity on the site. While they believe a house should employ simple structural solutions, they also aim, if possible, to advance the technology of house building. Since the firm builds houses as well as designs them, they can personalize and fit the houses to the sites while they are working.

Jersey Devil frequently uses materials that are made for some other purpose, since such objects can be cheaper than standard building materials. For example, on a recent house, they used prefabricated silos covered with precut siding and topped the composition with solar collectors sheathed with vinyl car roofing. They note that the resulting shapes are somewhat comical and that they aren't concerned with preconceived ideas of "good taste."

Their working methods are unusual. They travel to their sites and camp out while the building is under construction. Instead of conventional working drawings, they sketch right on the lumber or put up a trial element. If it doesn't work out for any reason, they tear it out and reuse it somewhere else. They believe this approach parallels methods used by painters and sculptors. Since they are in touch with their construction costs on a day-to-day basis, they can make periodic adjustments to the design to keep costs within original projections.

"Airplane" house designers were builders too

Project: *Airplane house, Colorado City, Colorado*
Designer/builder: *Jersey Devil Design/ Construction*
Date Completed: *1980*

The owners of this house, which has been dubbed the "airplane" house by its neighbors, wanted an open-plan, low-maintenance retirement home suitable for two people and expressive of their interest in aviation. They also needed workshop space for rebuilding automobile and airplane engines. Construction and materials costs had to be kept low without affecting the livability of the house. Solar heating was an obvious priority due to the abundance of sunlight in the Colorado climate and the extreme (usually 50°F) difference between day and night temperatures.

In response to these design requirements, the architects proposed a symmetrical, split-level structure whose winglike roof, hangar interior, industrial siding, and curved truss construction would make the aviator feel at home. The owner's airplane registration number—N62FL—is stenciled on the carport roof as a greeting to airborne friends.

The wedge shape of the ¼-acre (.1-hectare) site dictated a departure from the traditional rectangular plan and suggested more of a "solar diagram"— narrow and low on the north, wide and high on the south. Digging the house into the slope provided fill to berm the northeast and northwest walls. In contrast with the other elevations, the wide south facade is extensively glazed, providing a view, daylight, and passive solar gain. The house is 1256 square feet (117 square meters).

DESIGN FEATURES

The designers/builders used a group of energy-efficient, low-cost materials such as double-glazed fiberglass panels for the upper clerestory windows, corrugated asphalt panels for the siding and roofing, and operable windows that come with integral, adjustable sliding shutters. In response to an expansive clay soil typical of the eastern slope of the Colorado Rockies, they designed a concrete grade beam that can take the movement of this kind of soil. The floor slab is exposed as the finished floor surface, with an integral rust-red pigment in the concrete sealed with polyurethane.

DESIGN/MANAGE TECHNIQUES

Once the overall shape and characteristics were determined in concert with the owners, details and techniques were worked out on site. The construction was accomplished by the designers/builders, with the following exceptions:

1. The mechanical trades.

2. Foundations, which were subcontracted to a mason who owned aluminum forms, since these would provide a smooth-finished surface for the exposed concrete wall.

Design was done for a fixed fee of $6,000, which was equal to 10 percent of the estimated cost. Permit drawings were the only documents provided, and the job was accomplished without detail drawings or specifications.

Below: The plan for this Colorado house recalls the shape of an airplane.

Bottom: The exterior combines solar features with aeronautical imagery.

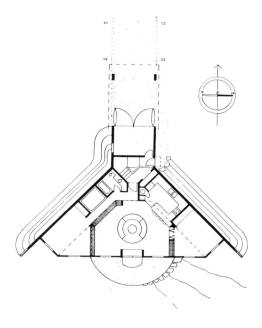

COST CONTROL

Final costs of $60,000 were under original estimates of $63,000, due mainly to a local recession resulting in lower material and mechanical subcontractor prices. Interior finish work was minimal and standard in contrast with the elaborately handcrafted built-ins typical of the firm. The designers/builders' site labor, amounting to approximately 25 percent of the total construction costs, was paid separately. In addition, the 10 percent overhead and profit fee was included in the construction agreement. This was paid in installments over the construction period. Travel expenses were paid separately for the builders to and from California. The cost breakdown was as follows:

Excavating	$ 1,000
Concrete	3,000
Plumbing	2,800
Electrical	2,500
Lumber and hardware	14,000
Corrugated roofing and siding	2,000
Windows	5,000
Kitchen	4,000
Insulation	1,200
Sheetrock and finish	2,500
Carpentry (rough & finish)	17,500
Contractor's fee	4,500
	$60,000

SCHEDULE

Ground was broken in June 1980, with completion by Thanksgiving. This met both owners' and designers/builders' time schedules for completion before winter snows.

A freeform pier defines the carport.

Windows are grouped geometrically and focus on the view.

LOUIS MACKALL & PARTNER/BREAKFAST WOODWORKS

Louis Mackall, Duo Dickinson
Branford, Connecticut

Kenneth Field, Louis Mackall

Architectural firm works closely with in-house woodworking shop

Since 1970, Louis Mackall has practiced as both architect and cabinetmaker. He frequently does both design and construction for his projects, and the cabinetmaker portion of his business, called "Breakfast Woodworks," will also do work designed by other architects.

In both design and construction, Louis Mackall & Partner enjoys a good reputation for quality work on complex projects. The firm stresses close ties between design and craft and is able to produce unusual work as a result. The practice divides projects into "ordinary" and "specialty" categories. Ordinary work includes routine carpentry and masonry work and the mechanical and electrical trades. Specialty items include woodwork, other than ordinary bases and trim, ornamental metalwork such as brackets for structural members and handrails, and unusual lighting fixtures.

The separation of these items from the general contract eases work flow, ensures good workmanship, and generally results in lower costs for the client, since prices for unusual items are frequently quoted at a premium because of the problems they pose for the contractor. Because of this, contractors will frequently welcome the separation of specialty items from their work.

Architect's house for sister incorporates inventions

Project: *Lucy Mackall house, Cambridge, Massachusetts*
Architects: *Louis Mackall & Partner*
Louis Mackall, Duo Dickinson
Woodworking: *Breakfast Woodworks*
Kenneth Field, Louis Mackall
Date Completed: *July 1982*

Louis Mackall's close relationship with the client enabled him to do a more fanciful design than perhaps might have been possible in the usual architect/client relationship.

Four major problems confronted the architect. His responses to them are listed here.

1. A tight lot with a not-small house: Entry vistas, cross axes, and high ceilings were employed to counter the narrowness of the lot on the inside of the house. Externally, the massing of the house was broken at the rear to create an elevated outdoor space.

2. A new house in a traditional neighborhood: The front elevation is simple and takes a cue from the surrounding buildings' scales and materials. Massing and fenestration become increasingly expressive toward the back of the house.

3. Desire for natural light, yet minimal exposure to neighbors: Skylights, two-story lightwells, and an elevated deck serve to get light in and keep eyes out.

4. Self-supporting residence: the design response includes well-insulated walls [9 inches (23 cm) thick], passive solar techniques (90 percent of glazing to the south, convection spaces, careful zoning of heat), and energy-efficient features (double glazing, weatherstripping, and air locks).

Besides these functional problems, the architects set themselves design expression goals. These were intended to reflect the personal characteristics of the inhabitant of the house. The means they used included invention of such details as the baseball visor overhang, the hanging master bedroom mirror, the countertop

The exterior of the Lucy Mackall house is simply detailed, using builder's standards, to fit in with the traditional neighborhood.

fireplace, the kitchen hood, the heart motif on the upper cabinets in the kitchen, and the glazed wall art piece between bedroom and bath. These items are all unique.

Lucy's apartment was 2112 square feet (196 square meters) including the basement. A rental unit took up 936 square feet (87 square meters).

DESIGN FEATURES

Curvilinear shapes such as the free-form partition wall, kitchen hood, cabinets, and baseball visor overhang are rich additions to the otherwise simple house forms. They were selected for separate design treatment because the architects were equipped to design and build them.

DESIGN/MANAGE TECHNIQUES

Louis Mackall & Partner worked with the general contractor, Breakfast Woodworks, and several other subcontractors to build the house. Breakfast Woodworks served as a business separate from the architectural firm, with Louis Mackall the common link. Breakfast Woodworks made the kitchen, the master bedroom wall, and the doors in direct contract with the owner. Other subcontractors made the hanging mirror and range hood. The general contractor, working on a cost-plus basis, built the house under the supervision of Louis Mackall & Partner. This work included the visor overhang.

One of the special concerns Mackall brings to every job is careful measurement of existing conditions. This enables him to accurately fabricate the elaborate cabinetwork in the shop with little need for on-site adjustments. While installing the work, the crew from Breakfast Woodworks camped out at the site for a week.

The architects charged only direct personal costs to the client because of the special family relationship.

COST CONTROL

The house was done at cost plus a fixed fee; specialty items were done on a fixed fee. Specialty items included the kitchen, bedroom wall and cabinets, doors, hanging mirror, range hood, and visor overhang.

A custom overhang adds whimsy to the rear grouping of french doors.

SCHEDULE

The original projected schedule of 6 to 7 months was revised to 9 to 10 months early in the design process. The actual construction time was 14 months.

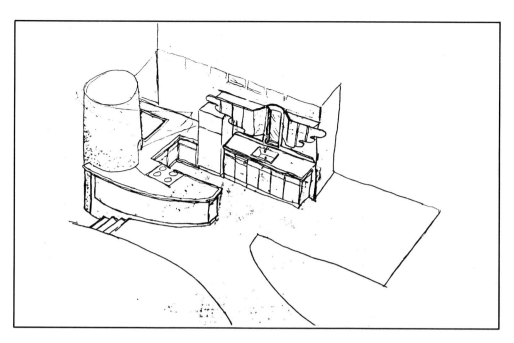

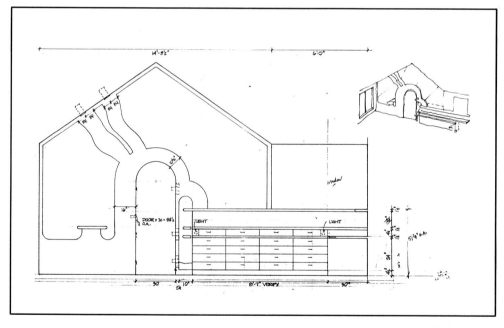

Top and above: Plans and details of the kitchen and bath were shown on a series of 11" × 17" (28 × 43 cm) drawings.

Top right: The exhaust fan above the cabinet was made by a sheet metal worker under separate contract.

Far right: All woodwork was fabricated in the architect's shop.

Right: The mirror in the bathroom was custom made and was procured separately by the architects.

SELLERS & COMPANY
Partners: David Sellers, Jim Sanford
Warren, Vermont

Architects work as part of building team

Describing the design approach of Sellers & Company, Jim Sanford comments: "The Kopit, Rosen, and Barrett houses are all jobs which we contracted ourselves. Doing this allows several advantages: elaborate sets of drawings are unnecessary, which saves time and money. The building does not need to be built on paper first. Because the architects are on the site, solutions to problem areas can be found using the actual three-dimensional reality; this affords the maximum amount of information needed to solve any problem. When difficult situations arise, the designer is on the site to guide the work. Phone calls, misunderstandings, and assumptions are all avoided.

"Opportunities to be creative often show themselves as the work evolves. With the design staff so closely related to the job, these can be taken advantage of. Also importantly, knowledge of building is thereby gained, which enables one to further evolve techniques used for other projects.

"Any work of art needs the maximum amount of guidance the artist can give it. Such first-hand participation in the evolution of a project inevitably gives it a character and personality no set of drawings or contractor would ever impart."

The architects do not believe that this kind of personal construction can be left to a third party to execute, citing historical examples such as Gothic cathedrals as their precedent for working things out on site. Their work indicates an interest in exposing structure and juxtaposing hand-built elements against manufactured elements. The size of the firm varies, depending on their workload.

Sellers & Company is interested in unique solutions to difficult building problems that the design/build concept allows them the freedom to do. The resulting efficiency also helps achieve savings in costs.

The interiors feature energy-efficient devices such as these louvers.

COST CONTROL

The owner sued the architects when costs exceeded the original budget by $12,000 over the original target of $48,000. However, he dropped the suit when he sold the house for $248,000.

SCHEDULE

The house was built over the course of a summer.

Flowing curves such as these are difficult to draw on paper.

Design for home/studio worked out using simple model

Project: *Nancy Barrett house, Damariscotta, Maine*
Architects: *Sellers & Company*
Date Completed: *1974*

This house was designed for a silversmith who planned to work and live in the house. The budget was $9,000 in 1974, and due to the absence of local building codes, the house was to be built without well, septic system, heating, or electricity. After a visit to the site, David Sellers agreed to build the house on site without drawings for a lump sum fee of $6,000, including materials. The crew camped on the site, and the client furnished all their food—mostly lobsters, clams, and pies.

The architects/builders were given a rudimentary program by the client, calling for a ground floor apartment, with a separate silversmith's studio, and two additional bedrooms. A roof deck was desirable five stories up to get a view of the ocean. The architect planned the house so a windmill could be located above it in the future.

DESIGN FEATURES

The design is shaped like a triangular tower with extending braces sheathed in plywood. These braces when sheathed form strong structural shapes and serve to brace the tall house against strong ocean windloads. Two of these buttresses enclose a two-story greenhouse. The third encloses the stair.

DESIGN/MANAGE TECHNIQUES

The design was entirely worked out in a simple model that required half a day to make. After the client approved a polaroid shot of the model, Sellers and five others of his group left Vermont at midnight to rendezvous with arriving lumber and concrete in Maine at 7:00 A.M. the next day. The six broke into three crews of two: the first framed the walls and buttresses, the second covered the framework with sheathing, and the third closed in windows, erected stairs,

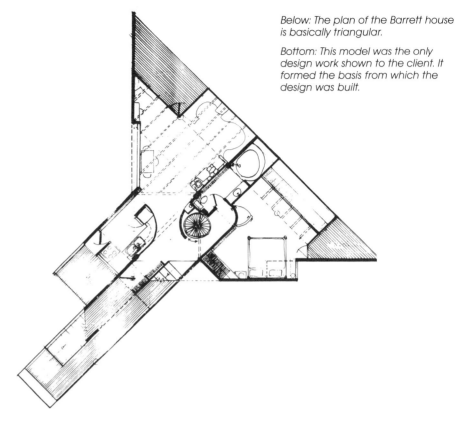

Below: The plan of the Barrett house is basically triangular.

Bottom: This model was the only design work shown to the client. It formed the basis from which the design was built.

and crafted details. If they were unsure of what to do, they let structural members stick out sufficiently to permit tidying up later when a solution presented itself.

The architects/builders are convinced that certain items—such as the stair—could not have been worked out on paper. In model form, they visualized it within the buttressed shape of the house. On site they built it as an outgrowth, covering it with acrylic glazing. Skylights were installed in complex geometric shapes,

serving to strengthen the acrylic sheets. At the time of this installation, glazing details for this type of skylight were new and untested. As a result, the initial installation leaked, and Sellers & Company replaced all of them some years later for the price of additional meals of lobster and pie.

The lack of thermal shutters made the house cold in winter and hot in summer. Movable insulation and louvers would have corrected the problem.

COST CONTROL

The original budget was not exceeded, but the lack of additional funds prevented the architects/builders from providing built-in storage or shading for the large south-facing skylight. Storage has been provided by the client on an ad hoc basis, but she is unsatisfied with the results because carpenters other than the original Sellers & Company crew did not detail the new installation in the same way.

No separate design fee was charged. The labor of the architects/builders was included in their set contract price of $6,000. The balance of the $9,000 budget went to other subcontractors or suppliers.

SCHEDULE

The house was essentially built within 10 days. Additions and changes are being made periodically by both Sellers & Company and others.

Above: A piece of curved plexiglass provides a dramatic top light to the stair.

Left: This corner view shows some of the angles that were determined on site.

MURPHY/JAHN
Partners: Charles F. Murphy, Helmut Jahn
Chicago, Illinois

Large Chicago firm specializes in highrise building

The Chicago firm of Murphy/Jahn specializes in large-scale commercial, institutional, and transportation buildings. Their staff of 120 includes architects, programmers, planners, landscapers, and interior designers. Conceptual design is done by Helmut Jahn, president of the firm, in collaboration with his partners. Contract documents are produced by teams assigned to each project.

Most of the firm's work is commissioned by commercial interests, and the architects must make use of available technologies and construction-industry work systems. Although the scale of their larger projects frequently requires innovative structural and mechanical solutions, sculptural forms are composed of standard materials cut to fit.

The design philosophy of Murphy/Jahn seeks to enrich functional solutions of technical and programmatic problems by using geometry, surface treatment, decoration, and historical reference to create a more people-pleasing environment.

Sympathetic builder erects geometric house on problematic lakefront site

Project: *House, Eagle River, Wisconsin*
Architects/Engineers: *Murphy/Jahn*
Builder: *F. Wiedenbauer & Sons, Eagle River, Wisconsin*
Date Completed: *1982*

This vacation house for a family of three provides 2500 square feet (232 square meters) of indoor living space and outdoor terraces on three levels. It is located on 3½ acres (1½ hectares) of lakefront property in northern Wisconsin. The house is sited in the center of a steeply wooded slope, affording views of the lake and opposite shore.

DESIGN FEATURES

The abstract geometric composition contrasts with the natural landscape. A 3-foot (91-cm) grid throughout is expressed on the exterior and the interior and left open or infilled with lattice, glass, or solid panels. An elevated classical cornice forms a base for the house above the round structural piers. The bridge access to the top level terrace frames views of the sky and lake.

DESIGN/MANAGE TECHNIQUES

Since Murphy/Jahn's practice is known for its design of skyscrapers, not wood vacation houses, they sought the expertise of a "master builder" capable of crafting a complex wooden structure. The local builder, F. Wiedenbauer, was challenged by both the site and the plans, and he worked cooperatively with the architects to realize their design.

The steep slope of the site raised several problems. A conventional approach to the construction of foundations was impossible due to the fact that a bulldozer couldn't negotiate the incline.

Above: The plans and axonometrics of this house in Eagle River, Wisconsin, were worked into this graphic design.

Right: Because of the unusual lakefront property a detailed soil boring plan was needed to analyze site problems and formulate decisions.

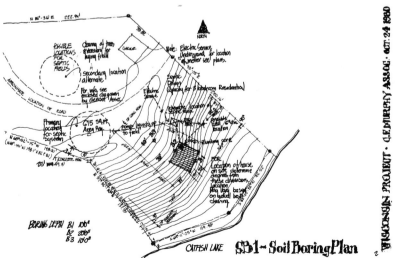

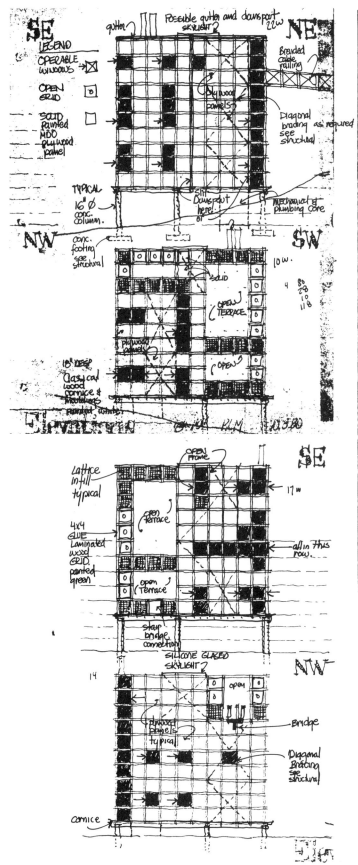

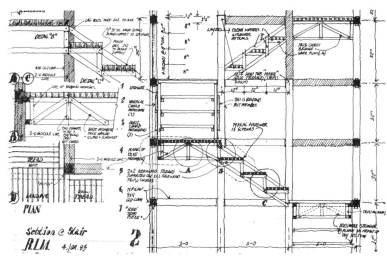

Opposite page left: All four elevations have decidedly different configurations, as shown in these freehand drawings.

Opposite page above: The stair element is skewed to the orientation of the house.

Opposite page below: Since the stairs play such a prominent part in this design, detailed sections and plans of them were required.

Above: Windows are set within a corner recessed into the exterior grid.

Since the house was poised above the landscape on piers, a backhoe was required to dig the pier holes. It was rolled down the hill by cable attached to a machine at the top of the hill. It had to be moved from hole to hole via the cable. Also impossible was the construction of a septic system on this slope, so it was built at the top of the hill and an ejector used below the house. All materials for the job had to be delivered by hand down the slope, since trucks had no access.

The 3-foot grid is the key element in this design. The builder worked out some of the details on site with the architects' approval. For example, the design called for fixed windows in front of recessed floor construction in some locations. These spandrels were to be painted charcoal gray to make them less visible from the outside. Since the painting of the structure behind the windows presented a problem (windows go in before painting), the builder requested that the window manufacturer supply all of them operable. The spandrel was then painted more easily when the windows were opened. It should be pointed out that there are other ways of doing this work, but the builder's suggestion made sense to the architects and was adopted.

The main lesson learned from this project is that it is essential for an architect unfamiliar with the scale of the project he/she is working on to develop a good relationship with a knowledgeable builder sympathetic to the design intent.

COST CONTROL

Actual costs exceeded budget estimates by 40 percent due mainly to site problems and owner changes during construction. The builder did the work with his two sons, subcontracting only excavating, mechanical, plumbing, and electrical specialties to others.

SCHEDULE

Construction took 21 months—longer than originally projected—but there were no time pressures on the job.

A two-story porch overlooks the view.

The careful jointing of wall and ceiling grids is apparent in this interior view.

FOSTER ASSOCIATES
Norman Foster
London, England

English architects are strong in creative programming and technological approaches

Norman Foster and his firm believe in integrating the "art" of architecture with the "business" of building buildings. This belief has led them to develop methods of working with an owner's program, budget, schedule, and quality goals to resolve problems and conflicts.

Foster Associates undertakes detailed studies with the owner of programs; distribution of reception, meeting, and work areas; and long- and short-term requirements and flexibility for choices, changes, and growth. While these studies are not architecture in the conventional sense, they do serve to bring out and analyze often conflicting requirements of owner needs versus building costs, servicing, and structure.

The office assigns a team to each project, and the discussions that lead to designs are focused on client needs and fulfillment of them in flexible and efficient ways. Most of the firm's work has been for industrial, commercial, or institutional clients who demanded cost-effective buildings quickly and within budget. The architects frequently use film or diagrammatic techniques to explain their unconventional approach to the user.

As a result of this approach, their buildings are characterized by a high-tech look that nonetheless is in tune with the environment. They have been inexpensive; yet their economy has been the result of appropriate technological innovation rather than cheapness of materials. The firm's stress is not on high technology so much as appropriate technology. For example, in a planning study for the Canary Islands, the firm proposed a type of house using labor-intensive mud-brick construction, combined with prefabricated kitchen and bath units from England.

Foster believes that prefabrication is suited to industrialized areas of the world—to an architecture that is shop built and site assembled. To this end, the firm has even worked with manufacturers to design individual components, based on prototype full-scale mockups. The goal is quality control from the manufacturer and efficiency of site assembly. Much of this approach is routine in the automobile and aircraft business.

The Foster firm's chief design concerns include:

· Integration of mechanical systems, structure, and skin, exposing them attractively when possible.

· Enclosure of a wide variety of functions under one roof to permit flexibility in the assignment of changing space needs.

· Spacious rooms and generous lighting to create controlled, pleasing spaces.

· Nonassertive buildings that fit and work with the environment.

· Provision of amenities such as swimming pools within work environments to provide employee benefits.

Building designed as machine to be adjustable

Project: *The Sainsbury Center for the Visual Arts, University of East Anglia, Norwich, England*
Architects: *Foster Associates*
Date Completed: *1977*

This building was worked out in close cooperation with the patrons, Sir Robert and Lady Sainsbury, and the owners and users, the University of East Anglia. The building had to accommodate viewing space for the collection, special exhibition space, the School of Fine Arts, a Senior Common room, and a restaurant. Its combined area is 6186 square meters (22,195 square feet).

Based on a worldwide survey of art galleries, an early decision was made to group all activities under a common roof to promote maximum mixing between the teaching of art history and the contemplation of works of art.

The building was to be sited in accordance with the university's original master plan on the axis of a newly created lake. The building was to serve as a meeting place and a short-cut route to academic areas.

DESIGN FEATURES

Natural lighting is automatically adjustable with motor-driven louvers. Open, flexible exhibit space uses relocatable display panels and dividers; gallery service routes do not disturb exhibits or users. Building elements are factory produced, with site work confined to assembly.

Of technical interest is a panel system integrated with the primary structure, thus enabling any part of the external walls and roof to be quickly changed to provide any combination of glazed, solid, or grilled aluminum panels. Prismatic towers and trusses house all services and toilets and provide an open raceway for lighting installations and maintenance. The entire inner wall is composed of adjustable perforated aluminum louvers. Additional opaque louvers related to glass roof lights are motorized and linked with internal light sensors to provide sophisticated light control.

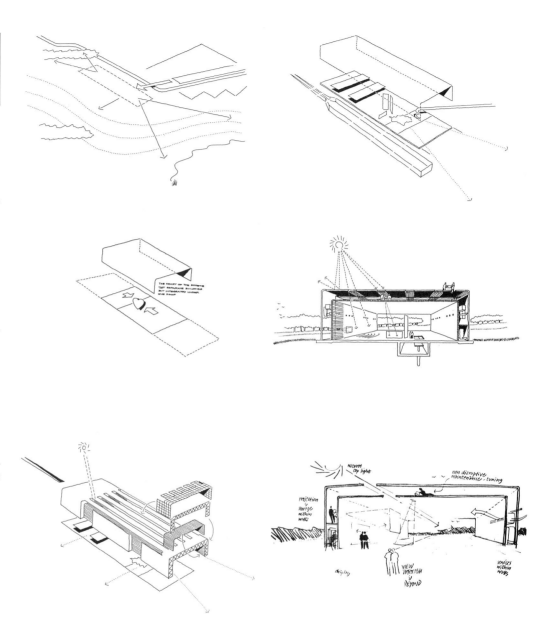

Conceptual sketches illustrate the evolution of the design concept for the Sainsbury Center, with the one on the bottom right summarizing the basic design principles.

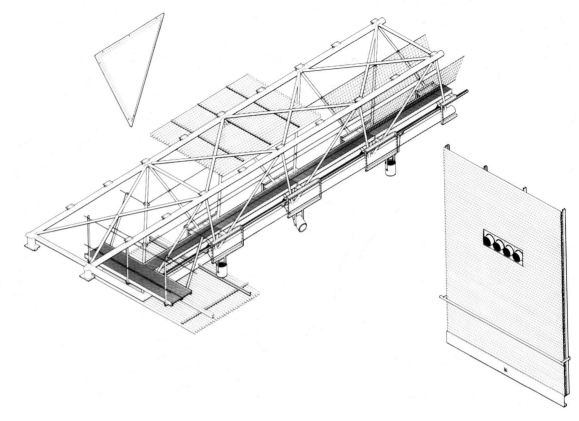

This kit of parts illustrates ceiling and wall components.

Structural elements and glass wall are shown in this kit of parts.

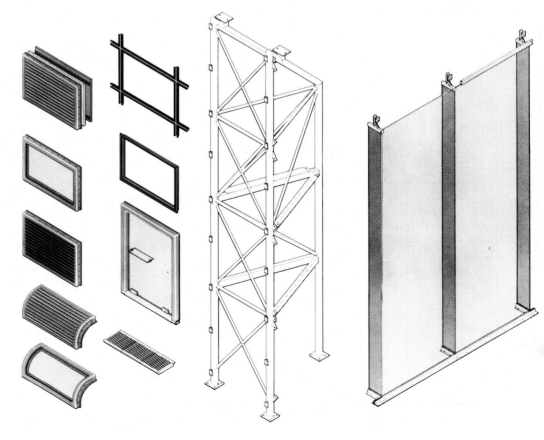

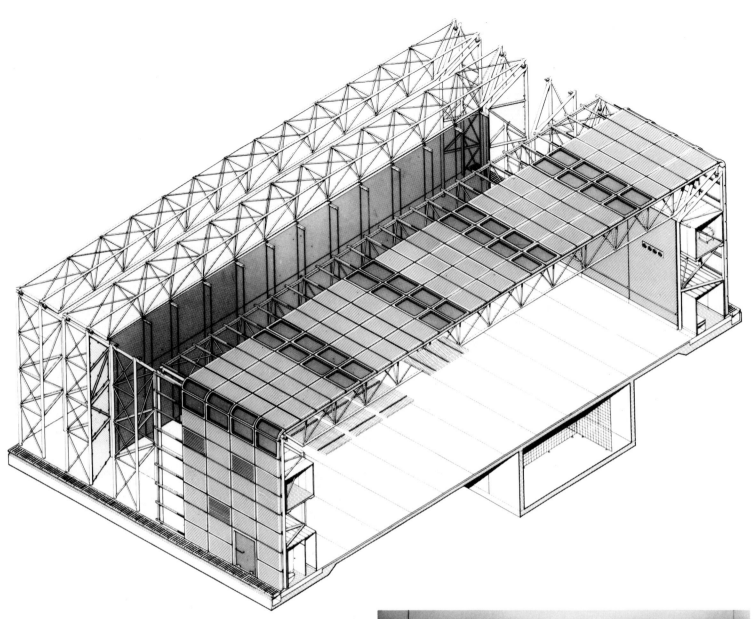

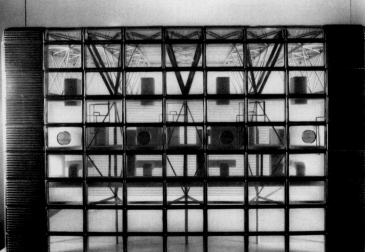

Above: This axonometric drawing illustrates the structural assembly of the Sainsbury Center.

Right: This was one of a series of models illustrating the structural and cladding concept.

DESIGN/MANAGE TECHNIQUES

In addition to the architects' unusual programming efforts with the clients and users, the architects used factory fabrication techniques and advanced technological systems. The building is basically a machine.

Early sketches clarified the planning ideas worked out with the patrons and client. Models were extensively used at first to study preliminary space layouts, structural alternatives, and cladding systems and, later, to explore service and structural ideas. Full-size models using proposed materials were developed to test a new sandwich cladding system. This led to the first application of aluminum molded in a manner usually associated with the plastics industry.

The key management concept here was the resolution of programmatic ideas with experimental solutions that required custom development on a trial-and-error basis.

COST CONTROL

Costs were substantially lower than those associated with comparable new galleries elsewhere in the world. This was largely due to the architects' extensive work with the manufacturers before construction began.

SCHEDULE

Construction time was two years—brief for this building type—due to the fact that various components could be fabricated at the same time.

Right: The roof system can be changed to fit a variety of solid and transparent panels.

Opposite page top: The long-span structural system provides dramatic ends open toward the view and circulation path.

Opposite page bottom: Interior lighting can be significantly changed depending upon the type of panel used and how the light is regulated through it.

Architects serve as management consultants

Project: *Willis Faber & Dumas offices, Ipswich, England*
Architects: *Foster Associates*
Date Completed: *1975*

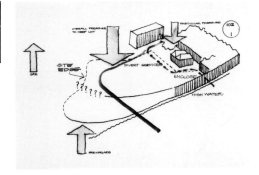

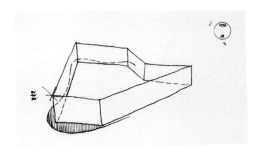

When the owners of a London-based insurance broker, Willis Faber & Dumas, decided to move their headquarters out of the City of London, they consulted Foster Associates with the idea of creating an enjoyable working environment for 1300 people. The program they presented to the architect called for a "distinguished building . . . not over-ambitious and yet not too pedestrian."

Of particular interest is the way in which the owner and architect developed the space program. Rather than presenting Foster with a site, detailed program, and budget, the owners came up with an initial statement outlining the company organization. Then, in collaboration, a joint management group was established, consultants were selected, and direct contacts were made between architects and the Board of Directors. The building takes up 20,500 square meters (73,553 square feet).

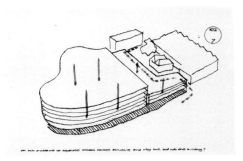

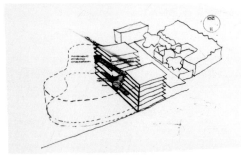

DESIGN FEATURES

The entrance area is linked to the rest of the building via escalators in a top-lit space. Priority was given to the comfort of the occupants. As a result, there is an inversion in the usual progression of quality standards from the entrance to workareas. The office areas feature polished aluminum ceilings, glare-free lighting, and carpeting, while the entrance areas are provided with utilitarian finishes such as rubber tile.

The building is a result of analysis of the advantages and disadvantages of highrise cellular office arrangements versus lowrise open plans. This analysis, combined with an examination of the site characteristics, led to an early decision to spread the building to fill the site.

The building makes extensive use of shop-fabricated elements for quality control and speed of construction. The only on-site wet trade required was for the

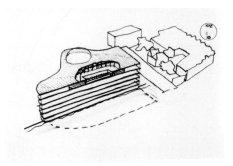

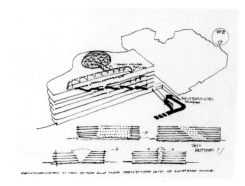

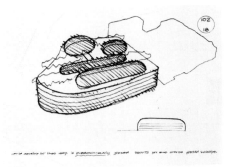

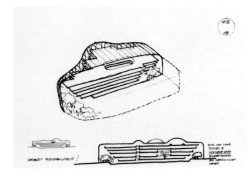

Conceptual sketches (8 out of 24 are shown here) trace the evolution of the design of the Willis Farber & Dumas offices.

GENERIC OFFICE TYPES

HIGHRISE/CELLULAR PLAN

1. Traditional office form evolved from rental basis that encourages poor space utilization.

2. Low net usable area to total due to inefficient plan form.

3. Generates corridor planning and wasted circulation space.

4. More circulation needed to communicate between floors.

5. Difficult interdepartmental communication.

6. Complicated management and supervision.

7. Difficult to provide a range of spaces that can accommodate changing work group sizes to house larger meetings. Tends to lead to crowded, small offices.

8. Partitions difficult to move and unable to change. Core areas tend to inhibit ease of reorganization.

9. Highrise construction is reflected in increased building costs and generally increased maintenance costs.

10. The tower form is only really appropriate to high-density urban situations. In the context of the small-scale jumbled development of Ipswich it is particularly inappropriate.

11. It is difficult to accommodate larger and more demanding spaces within the tower form. Hence the agglomeration of podium and low blocks in a typical development.

LOWRISE/OPEN PLAN

1. Office form developed from progressive design studies and organization and management-based background.

2. High net usable area to total efficient plan form.

3. Circulation space minimized. No corridors or wasted corners.

4. Traffic reduced as more people on one floor.

5. Better interdepartmental communication.

6. Better management and supervision.

7. High level of flexibility to reorganize layout, respond to changes in workflow, accommodate different sizes of groups for work or meetings.

8. Large open plan areas impose few constraints on reorganization of space.

9. Construction costs tend to be lower as do maintenance costs—reduced area of external wall. With same budget can spend higher proportion on improved working conditions.

10. Lowrise buildings easier to accommodate in small-town context.

11. Can accommodate large spaces within overall form of lowrise building.

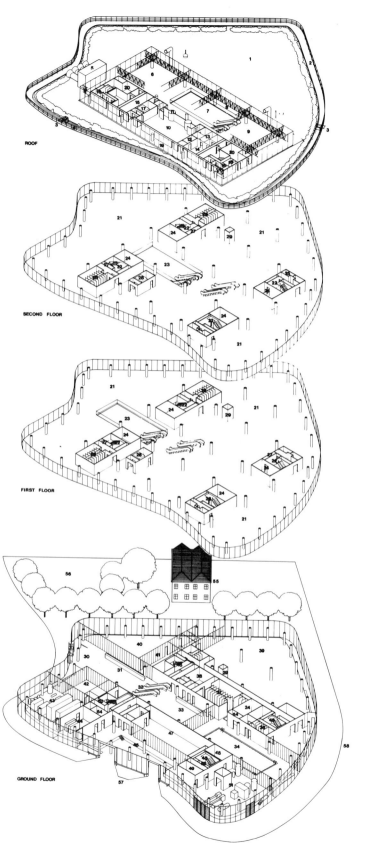

ROOF

SECOND FLOOR

FIRST FLOOR

GROUND FLOOR

*Exploded plan indicates central circulation on the ground floor;
services within the free-form perimeter; and the roof garden.*

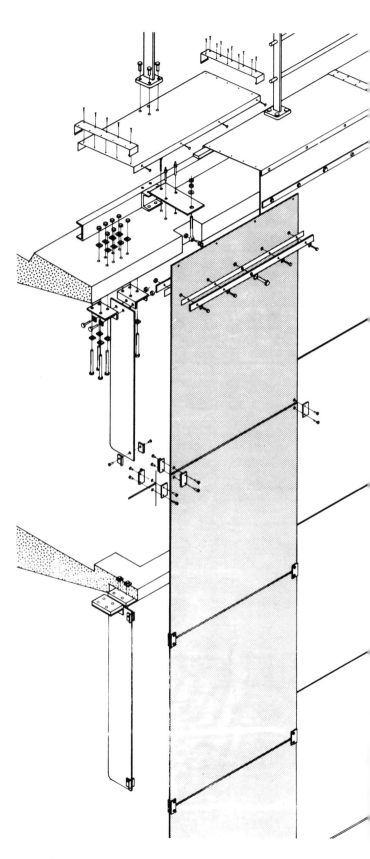

Glass was mechanically fastened to the projecting concrete slab.

At night, the interior illumination dissolves the reflective glass and reveals the ground floor mechanical equipment and the reflective metal ceiling of the upper floors.

concrete structure. As a consequence, construction was completed in two years. The low building with its small proportion of glass-to-floor area, high-efficiency lighting, and heavily insulated roof have yielded an energy-efficient building.

DESIGN/MANAGE TECHNIQUES

The management collaboration between owner and architect occurred before the purchase of the site and formulation of a program or budget. Real estate acquisition at that time was volatile enough to preclude a conventional prepurchase of the site before design was begun.

Detailed analysis went into development of the structure and the skin. The structural aim was a framework of concrete handsome enough to remain exposed. The skin was designed in the belief that most people are happier being able to see out. Since the building is deep, the amount of glass was increased, and systems were studied to combine transparency with acoustic and solar control. The glass is tinted for solar control and specially fastened to hang on the structure from clips. This technology was worked out with the glass manufacturer and the installer.

Of interest are the discussions between the owner's management and the architects about the principles of office planning, since they revealed the possibility of more open planning. Since some of the London-based staff were reluctant to move, special presentations were made, including 46 drawings by a newspaper cartoonist who put the proposals in an appealing light.

The architects billed on a time basis during the early consulting periods. This was combined with a negotiated percentage fee for the more conventional design work.

COST CONTROL

The architects combined analysis of generic office types (see box on page 129) with continuous financial appraisals, during which they compared minimum construction costs with on-going maintenance and energy costs. The building was within cost estimates

SCHEDULE

This was a crash program, in which a lot of the fabrication took place during the early stages of the project. These came together on site in a very short timespan. During this period, the architects did more management consulting than applying their design-based skills.

Above: The rooftop cafeteria looks out on a grassy garden.

Left: Interior vertical circulation is a strong design feature.

Initial phase of construction completed in nine months

Project: *IBM Technical Park, Greenford, Middlesex, England*
Architects: *Foster Associates*
Date Completed: *Phase 1: 1977*
Phase 2: 1979

In January 1977, IBM alerted Foster Associates to the possibility of a crash program to build a computer center, but did not give them a definitive direction until after site work had begun. Their program called for a 31,400-square-meter (112,662-square-foot) technical park set in open fields with open workplace planning units within the building. This program identified movement patterns on the site and allocated space for future building activity. Computer machine areas, education and administrative spaces, offices, workshop, storage, and reception were all to be grouped under one roof for future flexibility. This idea has proved effective, since many functions have been expanded or contracted within the overall building perimeter.

DESIGN FEATURES

Features include modular component assembly system; capability for changes via a big open space; deep plan with a variety of secondary services, fixtures, finishes, and machines to tailor specific locations to specific services; a prefab approach to detailing; inclusion of clever gadgets such as new security and phone systems.

DESIGN/MANAGE TECHNIQUES

Despite the client's initial ideas about construction and schedule, the architects reviewed component building systems and demonstrated to the client that a deep-plan, variable-height (but with a constant roof line) building could provide more efficient and flexible space and better quality with no cost or time penalty. The architects had previous experience with the design of expandable buildings for this owner and were able to bring this experience to good use in the new facility. They used simple methods such as sketches (see page 134) to demonstrate their planning ideas.

The reflective glass wall of the IBM building works well with its park setting.

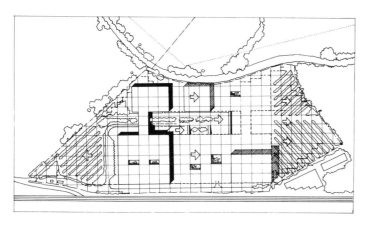

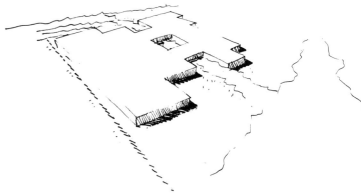

Above: IBM site plan illustrates expansion possibilities.

Right: These expansion analysis sketches were used to explain the design concept to the client. Captions read: . . . (top) "make random incremental growth to fill corners" (middle)". . . and create courts . . . external and the usual deeper spaces only if appropriate . . . or atriums—internal top lit spaces" (bottom) ". . . respecting the relationship of floor levels across the site does not preclude a total development of varying heights."

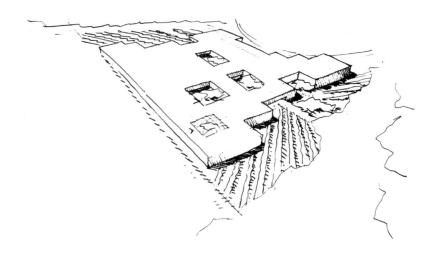

COST CONTROL

The budget for the initial phases of construction was open ended since schedule was a more vital concern. The budget evolved as various systems were reviewed. Late phases were completed according to rigidly controlled cost budgets.

SCHEDULE

The first phase of the building was completed in nine months, a very short period for a building of this type with such internal systems complexity. Built-in flexibility has been demonstrated by relocation of office spaces to accommodate more machinery, numerous interdepartmental moves, and the introduction of new security, communications, and data processing systems.

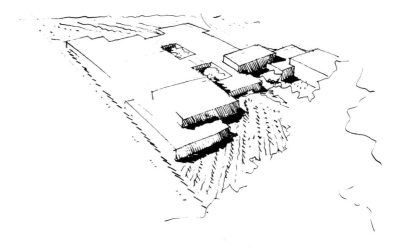

Below: This detail shows wall assembly.

Right: Service functions such as window washing and delivery bays are dramatized rather than hidden.

Bottom: Interiors are simple and industrial.

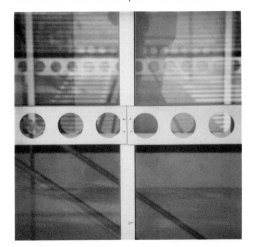

WILLIAM P. BRUDER, ARCHITECT, LTD.
New River, Arizona

Architect's design preferences necessitate close on-site coordination with owners, builders

On many of his projects, William P. Bruder works intensively with his clients and their programs, and he frequently involves them in the actual building process. Some projects have had budgets low enough to mandate a form of owner participation in the construction stage. Bruder encourages this sort of owner labor and tries to make use of the particular skills that the owner possesses. For instance, in the Karber Air Conditioning building (see pages 143–144), the carefully constructed ductwork is an expression of their trade and shows off their skill. To give Maude's—An Eating Establishment (see pages 137–139) the personal stamp of the owners, the architect selected nostalgic photos from the owners' heirloom family album and had them enlarged, mounted, and displayed to good effect.

Where possible, Bruder also encourages his own involvement in the selection of the site, because he believes he can give insight into the kind of ambience the owner is looking for.

The architect's plans are richly varied and frequently combine curves and angles. The influence of Frank Lloyd Wright's work in the Southwest is evident; the combination of natural materials with industrial-looking sheet metal walls and ductwork is distinctively Bruder's own idiom.

Banners, bare bulbs, heirloom prints personalize gourmet lunch shop

Project: *Maude's—An Eating Establishment, Prescott, Arizona*
Architect: *William P. Bruder, Architect, Ltd.*
Date Completed: *1978*

This project involves an interior space for a gourmet lunch shop, Maude's—An Eating Establishment. The main problem was to develop a sense of scale and individual character within a long, high space—588 square feet (55 square meters)—on a budget of $7,000.

DESIGN FEATURES

The solution uses repeated modules of exposed light bulbs and translucent, brightly colored fabric banners to establish the perceived height of a 7-foot, 4-inch (2-meter) ceiling instead of the actual 14-foot (4-meter) height. These banners are aligned symmetrically on either side of a central aisle, above which is a mechanical duct of shiny galvanized metal.

The lighting treatment is an inexpensive system of bare bulbs. The bulbs are high enough over the tables to be out of diners' vision, and hanging fabric baffles shield customers from bulbs lighting adjoining spaces. The banner/light system also provides a pattern of diagonal shadows on the gray walls. Photo artwork and plants in hanging metal cylinders further define the scale of the space and add design interest.

DESIGN/MANAGE TECHNIQUES

The owners hired the architect prior to leasing the space. By doing so, they were able to evaluate the architectural aspects of potential spaces. This proved key to meeting budget and time goals. For example, on a first visit to the eventual location, a beautiful, but well-worn, turn-of-the-century pine plank floor hidden by carpet and linoleum was discovered. During construction this floor was sanded and sealed to a fine effect, thereby saving the cost of new flooring. The architect also helped the owners actually build the project.

Bare bulbs providing illumination for the space are baffled by banners in Maude's.

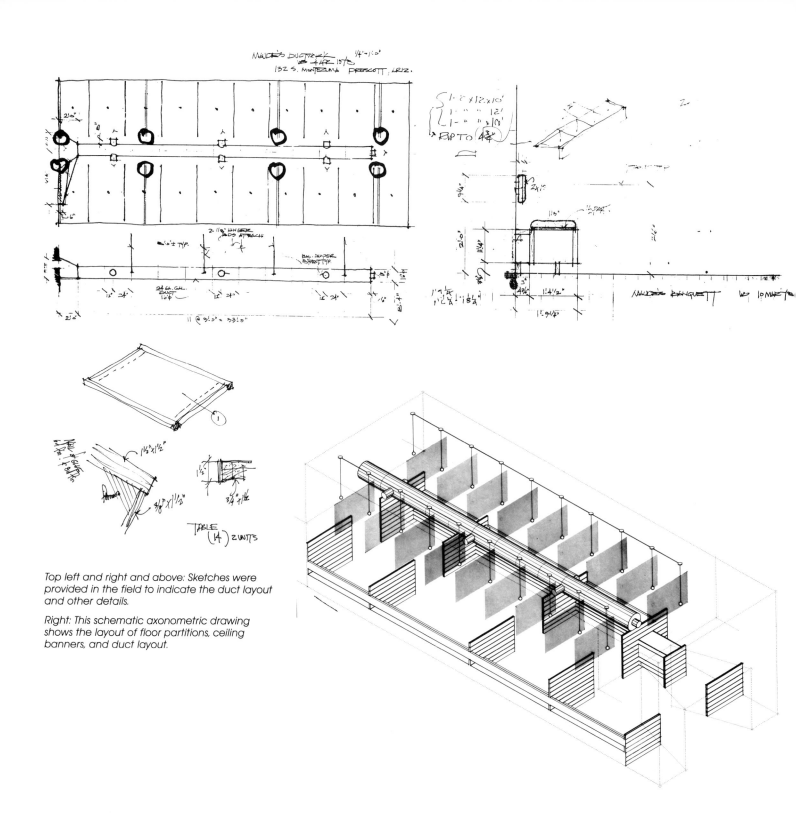

Top left and right and above: Sketches were provided in the field to indicate the duct layout and other details.

Right: This schematic axonometric drawing shows the layout of floor partitions, ceiling banners, and duct layout.

Office addition displays owner's craft

Project: *Karber Air Conditioning Company office, Phoenix, Arizona*
Architect: *William P. Bruder, Architect, Ltd.*
Date Completed: *1977*

The program was to provide an office facility for Karber Air Conditioning Company, a small contractor. Primary needs included a public reception area, five management offices, a central drafting/work room, and a conference room. The budget was very limited and much work was to be done by the owners. The site—2000 square feet (186 square meters)—was adjacent to their existing shop housed in a prefabricated metal building. The neighborhood was an old central Phoenix industrial area.

DESIGN FEATURES

The building was designed as a showplace for the owner's craft. The design features an arched barrel vault of double corrugated galvanized metal skins [20 × 40 feet (6 × 12 meters)] which becomes the main focus of the building. The metal vault structure, typically used for conveyor belt covers, is an economical, weatherproof spanning element. Natural daylight is provided through north- and south-facing clerestories. The mechanical ducts are exposed within the vault and painted bright orange. The drafting/work room and conference space are housed there, and built-in storage and work stations are provided.

Adjacent to the main space are five offices and a reception area enclosed by sandblasted concrete block walls. Interior partitions of fir plywood are combined with exposed wood roof framing and a 4-foot (1-meter) wide edge skylight, which provides natural highlighting of the cinder aggregate walls. An interior clerestory above the door extends each office into the main vaulted space.

All furniture was designed or selected by the architect, who also provided graphics, artwork, and landscape design.

The materials of the exterior express the nature of the client's air conditioning company.

DESIGN/MANAGE TECHNIQUES

Bruder was approached about the project after the owner had served as a sub-contractor on a remodeling job designed by him. After an initial client request to "draw blueprints for a building permit," the architect made an effort to understand the capabilities of the owner's craft and resources along with more traditional program needs. Since the architect was a one-man operation at the time, he was able to work closely with the owner and refine many details on site or in the owner's metal shop during construction.

The architectural fee was set on a percentage of the projected cost of the project. The architect has learned in dealing with many owner/builders over the years to quote a lump sum fee based on 12 to 15 percent of the projected fair market value of the building project, instead of the owner's cost. This gives him a fair return for his services, while giving the owner more for his involvement than conventional methods of building with contractor's expenses and overhead. The architect notes that the owner/builder must be carefully evaluated with regard to their goals and what they expect from the architect.

COST CONTROL

Since the owner provided his own labor and obtained many favors through contractor contacts, the cost was kept to a minimum.

SCHEDULE

Money was more critical than time, and the owner tailored the construction schedule to maintain reasonable progress. The job was completed within a year.

Left: Finishes are durable and simple. The plywood to the left of the reception desk is ordinary fir, frequently used for sheathing and covered with other finishes.

Below: The interior ductwork is also a showpiece of the firm's business.

ALDO ROSSI
Venice, Italy

Architect designs work within Italian vernacular building tradition

Aldo Rossi works within the building traditions of northern Italy, which are based on solid walls of stone or brick pierced by simple openings, large covered spaces, and open porticoes. Rooms are organized simply, often on axis or within a formal composition.

This design kit of parts enables the architect to do a large volume of work with very few drawings, which merely outline the conceptual scheme without a lot of details. Rossi relies on local building traditions and craftsmanship to get things built correctly. He feels his designs are so straightforward that there is no need to elaborate on them with detailed instructions to builders.

His office generally includes two or three assistants, and he will form temporary partnerships for selected projects.

Floating theater is built by local shipyard

Project: *Il Teatro del Mondo, Venice, Italy*
Architect: *Aldo Rossi*
Date Completed: *1979*

The Teatro del Mondo was commissioned as part of the 1979 Venice Biennale Exposition. It was a floating theater, part of a Venetian tradition of pavilions on the water dating from the 16th century. Historically, these were temporary structures (as this was—it is now demolished) in which performances and spectacular events took place. Various forms such as triumphal arches or towers were built, and fountains or fireworks were used as part of the display.

The program for the structure called for a closed multipurpose theater in the round, with a seating capacity of 250, in which performances, meetings, and talks could be held.

Drawings of Il Teatro del Mondo illustrate the planar simplicity of the building.

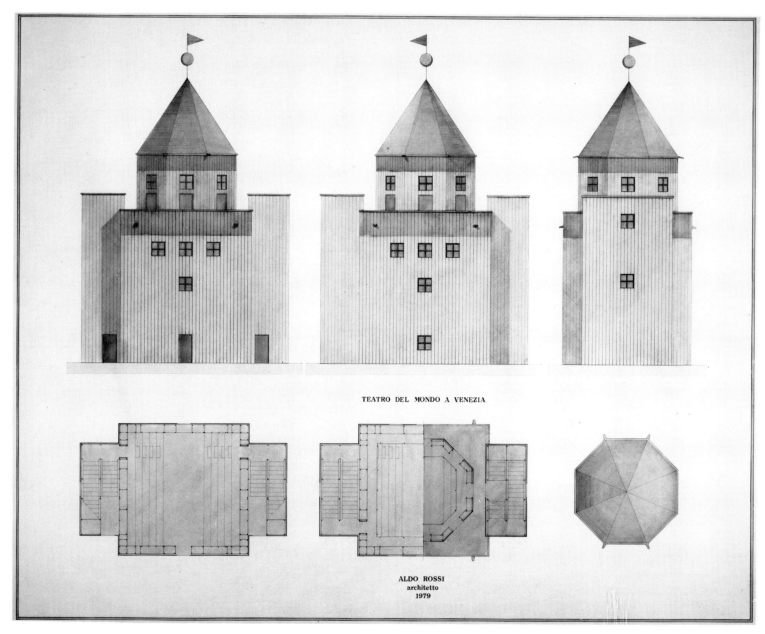

TEATRO DEL MONDO A VENEZIA

ALDO ROSSI
architetto
1979

DESIGN FEATURES

There are three tiers of stepped balconies on each side of a central stage. The bottom two balconies are square in plan. This reflects the volume of the building, which is a cube 9.5 meters (31 feet) square in plan and 11 meters (36 feet) high. Over this is an octagonal volume topped by a pyramidal roof. Two smaller rectangular volumes flank the central cube and contain the stairs, which lead to a terrace. On the stage and gallery levels there are three lines of windows, framing views of the sea and Venetian landmarks.

DESIGN/MANAGE TECHNIQUES

Simple conceptual drawings were given to a local shipyard, which fabricated the wood sheathing over a pipe scaffolding that remained the basic structure within the building. Ordinary black pipe scaffolding, fastened with gold-colored clips, was used. The building was constructed with joinery and details commonly used in boat building.

A negotiated lump-sum fee arrangement was agreed to for the architect's work.

COST CONTROL

Costs were within original estimates.

SCHEDULE

The building was completed on schedule.

Top: An industrial gangplank provided pedestrian access to the floating theater.

Above: The barge on which the theater was transported also served as its foundation.

Construction techniques build on local traditions

Project: *Secondary School, Broni, near Pavia, Italy*
Architects: *Aldo Rossi, Gianni Braghieri*
Date Completed: *1982*

This secondary school is located in a small town outside Pavia in northern Italy within a grouping of schools housing other grade levels. Students use the cafeteria and gymnasium of a nearby high school.

The program called for a theater/auditorium and a series of classrooms and supporting spaces. Rossi and temporary partner Gianni Braghieri organized the classrooms in a square enclosing a green courtyard in which the theater/auditorium was placed and connected to the perimeter by a corridor and open, but covered walkways.

DESIGN FEATURES

The theater/auditorium in the center of the school is octagonal on a circular base, covered by a steel-framed roof sheathed with wood. The covered walkways and the corridor leading to this building bisect the courtyard into four quadrants. Circulation to the perimeter classrooms and offices is via a corridor surrounding the courtyard.

The entrance to the school is through a pedimented open porch. At the center of the pediment is an exterior clock of the type frequently found on the outside of public buildings.

Left: Conceptual sketches of the secondary school in Broni were done in color.

Below: The exterior detailing of the school resembles that of many local vernacular buildings. The placement of the windows, colors, and the central octagonal element distinguish the building.

DESIGN/MANAGE TECHNIQUES

The buildings are of reinforced concrete and concrete block that are stuccoed and painted white. The structure of the roofs is steel sheathed with wood and metal painted light blue. Windows are made of standard wooden sections painted blue.

An article in the Italian press on the school compares it with two adjacent prefabricated schools, which are reviewed unfavorably. In rebuttal to this criticism, the director of the company that manufactured the two schools described the Rossi/Braghieri school as "using pre-historic techniques and with construction dragged out over a lengthy period."

An important conflict of building philosophies is raised by this discussion of techniques for the two schools with similar programs built at the same time. The director of the prefabricated building company is correct in noting the greater length of field fabrication time required for the Rossi/Braghieri school. However, the building industry in general and in Italy in particular is at heart traditional, and it is not necessary to use sophisticated prefabrication techniques on as simple a building as a school. The reason for this is economics. Simple, traditionally built structures are as cheap or cheaper than prefabbed ones. Therefore Rossi's approach is valid since it stresses simple, traditional detailing that local tradesmen understand.

COST CONTROL

The building was on budget.

SCHEDULE

Although the building took longer to build on site than the adjacent prefabricated schools, construction time was within that projected.

Above: Window and door openings are simple and easy to build.

Left: Although the form of this multipurpose assembly room is unusual, the placement of openings and stepped areas does not require unusual construction techniques.

JOHN ANDREWS INTERNATIONAL
Palm Beach, Australia

Architects emphasize process in completing their designs

John Andrews International is noted for its large commercial, institutional, and planning projects. A book on Andrew's work, *Architecture: A Performing Art,* was published by Oxford University Press in 1982. In it, Andrews stresses the processes he uses to convince people to build what he believes will ultimately be the best solution for their building program. He thinks that "performance" in architecture involves not only the definition of the problems and their sensible solutions, but documentation, wheeling and dealing, and supervision of the project.

In Andrew's words, architecture is "taking the responsibility—a responsibility that stays with an architect for the whole of his life with everything he builds; the performance of making sure you can survive under these circumstances which means fighting with builders, becoming more and more involved with the legal profession, paying insurance and trying to make sure you do not get wiped out by a decision that was maybe made by you, or maybe not, and made at some time long erased from your memory but for which you are still responsible. This performance is absolutely real and in these terms architecture is *certainly* a performing art."

Local technology, unskilled labor used to assemble prefabricated rural house

Project: *Andrews house, Eugowra, Australia*
Architects: *John Andrews International*
Date Completed: *1980*

This farmhouse, built on a 3000-acre (1200-hectare) site in the Australian countryside, was the first house built by John Andrews. Before designing it, the architect looked at vernacular houses in this sparsely populated area and discovered that many of them were based on Georgian cottages introduced by settlers from England in the 18th century. The classical roots of the local houses show in their symmetry but the hot climate led to modifications such as encircling verandas and ventilated pitched roofs. Further changes were brought about by economic considerations that encouraged the use of wood and corrugated iron instead of the stone and slate of England.

In designing this house, Andrews sought to extract the best aspects of the vernacular and demonstrated that a prefabricated building, adaptively designed and available from manufacturer's catalogs, was appropriate to house construction.

The house—3500 square feet (325 square meters) includes the garage—is occupied by Andrews and his wife. An existing nearby farmhouse provides for their children and guests.

Above: In the plan of the Andrews house the main living areas are grouped toward the sun.

Right: Corrugated metal was used extensively for the exterior cladding.

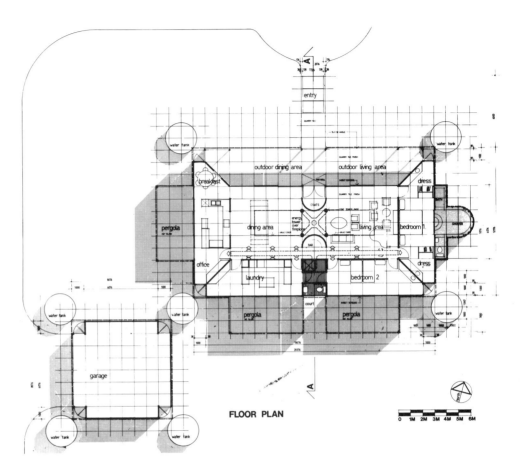

FLOOR PLAN

0 1M 2M 3M 4M 5M 6M

DESIGN FEATURES

The layout is formal and axial with a broad covered veranda on the north. The master bedroom is at one end, with the kitchen at the other and a dominant fireplace/chimney/watertower in the middle flanked by dining and living areas. This tower rises high above the ridge and supports a water storage tank, chimney, and lightning rod. It is designed to take solar collectors and a windmill (to raise the water collected in seven large tanks located under the eaves at the corners of the main house and in a nearby car shelter). Strong visual expression of these tanks signifies the importance of collecting rainfall in these often drought-stricken areas.

Climate was a controlling factor in this

design. The winters are moderate with occasional frosts at night, and the summers are hot and dry. The orientation of the rooms takes advantage of prevailing breezes and also induces them by the placement of the cool corner tanks and adjacent diagonal walls that direct air flow into the house. The interior ceilings follow the roof pitch, so warm air flows up these pitches and is released through the open ends of the barrel vaults that cap the long hipped roof. There are few doors within the house so sunlight and breezes move freely.

A striking feature is the bathroom alcove off the bedroom at the east end of the house, which is formed of curved transparent acrylic in a steel frame.

including the kitchen. The design for this new work was accomplished rapidly, using 8½″ × 11″ (22 × 28 cm) sheets of drawings. Bids were obtained on the job. Construction began immediately and continued with other work already underway.

While demolition and rough construction took place, design of architectural details, cabinetwork, marble floor paving pattern, fireplace facade, and electrical work were completed. These items were bid separately with subcontractors preselected based on their quality/cost reputation on previous projects managed by the architect. Control was exercised over the selection of materials and the quality of workmanship of all trades.

The architect's objectives in construction managing the work were as follows:

· Control over tradesmen: Through professional contacts, the architect located an old-world craftsman to recreate the wet plaster ceiling moldings that were lost when old plaster ceilings were replaced with sheetrock.

· Control over materials selections: Sources for marble and granite floors, fireplace facade, and countertops were researched for quality and price and orders placed directly with suppliers.

· Control over technical detail: To make the new air conditioning ductwork and equipment fit into existing tight spaces required hours working with the HVAC subcontractor seeking creative solutions to difficult problems.

· Control over quality of execution: Daily on-site coordination between architect and tradesmen helped resolve minor field problems as they arose. For example, tile jointing patterns in the platform bathtub were controlled and standard sheetrock casing beads were used to recreate original plaster detail profiles on the staircase.

COST CONTROL

Daily consultation with the subcontractors allowed close monitoring of costs; this was essential since the scope of work could not be defined in advance. It also permitted direct competitive bidding and negotiation with preselected subcontractors and suppliers. By dividing the project into multiple contracts with tradesmen

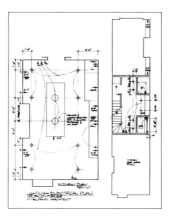 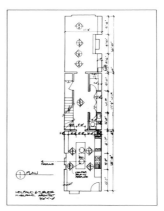 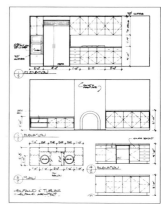

and suppliers it was possible to save the overhead and profit markups of a general contractor.

SCHEDULE

Construction was completed in seven months. This was fast work since demolition and reconstruction of the ground floor were not begun until the third month. On-the-spot design work combined with construction management by the architect aided the schedule.

Top: The basic layout was detailed on 8½″ × 11″ (22 × 28 cm) sheets.

Above: The new kitchen incorporates an existing fireplace.

TAFT ARCHITECTS

Partners: John J. Casabarian, Danny Samuels, Robert H. Timme
Houston, Texas

Architects use inexpensive materials and techniques for design impact

This partnership of young architects uses a number of unconventional decorative and presentation techniques in their work. Since much of their current work must be built at market rates, they use tile on the exterior of their buildings, shaping patterns to dramatize entrances or important spaces within. Building identification is done by designing and fabricating such features as the YWCA medallions (see page 14 top) in their own shop below the office. Stenciling is another inexpensive and effective design tool that the firm employs occasionally, such as on the West Indies house (page 160) and the Galveston renovation (see page 165).

Features such as these often become a firm's signature. Stenciling in the West Indies house was payment for the use of the house for a firm vacation, an unusual house gift. The YWCA medallions were contributed, as was the base stencil for the Galveston renovation.

In addition to these techniques, the architects use color and trim pieces inside and out to define and accent walls and ceilings.

The use of three-dimensional constructions and models as an extension of traditional drawing techniques is an important aspect of Taft Architects' design approach. At the initial stages of a project, small-scale diagrammatic models are used to investigate various design possibilities. As a project develops, larger models are used to explore more detailed aspects of space through the use of materials, colors, and patterns.

The diorama, or "shadow box" technique, was developed during the design process for the Houston YWCA in 1979, as a means for studying specific spatial characteristics of the central space. The forced perspective used in the model encourages the viewer to become more involved with the space. Multiple vanishing points are introduced in this construction, with the resulting depth shortened to about one-sixth the actual proportional distance.

Vernacular techniques used to build Caribbean house

Project: *Talbot house, Nevis, West Indies*
Architects: *Taft Architects*
Date Completed: *1981*

The program was a residence for a Vermont maple syrup farmer, his wife, and child on the island of Nevis in the West Indies where they plan to cultivate citrus fruit. Nevis is a small volcanic island in the Lesser Antilles, and buildings on the island are constructed from cut native stone and wood and painted in complementary colors. Roofs are either red or green, which are locally perceived as neighborly colors. Massing of the buildings is formal in organization. The main existing cultural influence on the architecture of the island is from the British colonial period.

The house is located on the former site of the main house of a plantation. The site—3116 square feet (290 square meters) on 10 acres (4 hectares)—is half way up Nevis Peak overlooking the Caribbean Sea on axis with a stately mango tree and cistern from the original plantation.

DESIGN FEATURES

The plan is composed of four cut stone two-story structures defining a central pavilion. Exterior spaces between these stone structures form four terraces. The ground floors of the corner structures serve as garages and workrooms, with a 35,000-gallon cistern located between them below the central living area. On this main level, three of the stone corner elements are bedrooms and the fourth is the kitchen.

The plan organization allows for views in all directions. Oversize casement windows permit cross ventilation in all spaces, regardless of the direction of the breeze, which is variable on the island. Since there is no electricity, power for lighting, food preparation, and refrigeration is provided by kerosene.

The exterior wood is painted complementary red-orange and blue-green, with lighter values used on the stone structures and darker values used for the

Brightly contrasting colors reflect vernacular traditions of the West Indies.

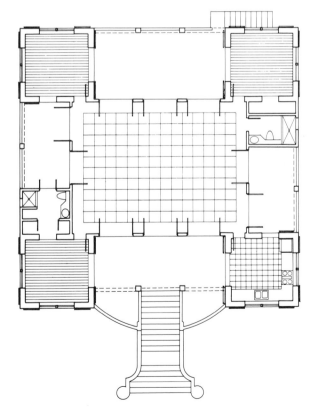
The four corner pavilions house three bedrooms and the kitchen.

central pavilion. Within, each room is painted in a different pair of complementary colors. Bands of floral patterns are hand stenciled at the top of each room.

DESIGN/MANAGE TECHNIQUES

Since Taft Architects were working in an area of the world where sophisticated construction techniques are unknown, the architects sensibly decided to employ local construction techniques and materials. The cut stone for the corner pavilion was found on site, left over from the earlier plantation. In addition to found materials such as this, local labor was used on tasks familiar to them, such as the construction of wood roofs and their cladding with corrugated metal and the erection of load-bearing stone exterior walls, floor slabs, and foundations. Other details such as interior plastering and wood floors were also locally understood and economically installed.

An important design feature within is the hand stenciling at the juncture of the roof and the walls, which was done by the architects.

COST CONTROL

Costs were negotiated with the local builder at the same time the materials palette and fabrication techniques were researched. Costs are comparable with other house construction on the island.

SCHEDULE

There were no scheduling problems during the construction period.

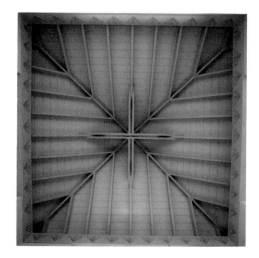

Above: Transoms provide ventilation when doors are closed.

Left: The pattern of the ceiling beams is surrounded by a frieze. The color of the stenciling varies from room to room.

Ornamental entrances provide portals to YWCA's recreational world

Project: *Masterson Branch YWCA and Metropolitan Administration Building, Houston, Texas*
Architects: *Taft Architects*
Date Completed: *1982*

The program for this YWCA building called for the immediate construction of offices, day care and children's play areas, a multipurpose gym, and an outdoor pool designed for future enclosure. A third multipurpose recreational room is planned. The Y's needs called for two different kinds of space—small ones for offices, lounges, and lockers and larger ones for sports.

The site backs a parkland on the south, which is accessible from the building. Vehicular access is from the north, where the site faces the street. The site is small—forcing the architects to line up parking areas directly on the street and to align the east and west ends of the building near the property line.

DESIGN FEATURES

Taft Architects designed the building to present different looking facades on the long north and south property lines. The north side, facing the street and the parking lot, is long and linear, ornamented with a pattern of terra-cotta tiles and two shades of stucco. The south side, facing the park and two major traffic arteries, is broken into separate pavilions, which are light colored against the dark tile of the linear north half of the building.

Variegated ornament such as the dark terra-cotta tile, colored stucco, and strips of blue tile trim distinguish the exterior and emphasize two major and one minor entrances.

Interior ornament echoes the exterior and is geometric, making use of traditional features such as chair rails as spring lines for moldings that outline doorways and recesses.

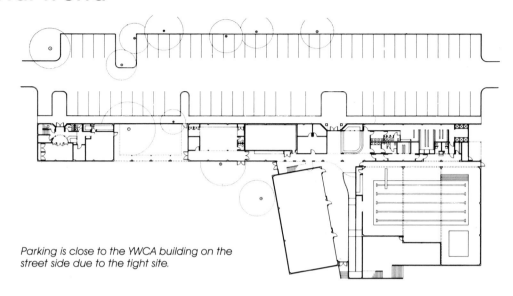

Parking is close to the YWCA building on the street side due to the tight site.

End walls are tiled in an irregular manner, and other materials are used to provide an inexpensive and interesting pattern.

DESIGN/MANAGE TECHNIQUES

A low budget and the requirement that this work be publicly bid forced the architects to concentrate their creative efforts on inexpensive ornamental patterns that would designate important areas and circulation points. A combination of tile and stucco was applied to the steel frame and stud structure, relating windows and door openings to the functions within the building. The architects also chose to emphasize with color such mundane functional items as air grilles, sound-absorbing materials, structural beams, and glazed overhead doors. They fabricated the cornerstone YWCA medallions flanking the entrance sign in their tile-making shop.

An important aspect of their design presentation to the client was a series of dioramas, which they call "stiff drawings." These are boxes about a foot deep (see right) that show the interiors in compressed perspective with a series of cutout cardboard planes. These seemingly fanciful abstractions were of value in presenting their ideas to a group of largely lay clients unaccustomed to visualizing conventional plans and elevation drawings.

COST CONTROL

Square-foot costs were within original projections. Ceramic tile made in the architects' shop was paid for separately.

SCHEDULE

The use of conventional structural and finishing techniques enabled the building to be completed on schedule.

Top: Dioramas like this one were used to show clients, who are unused to visualizing spaces, how the building will look. (Actual area shown below.)

Above: Interior design interest is provided by bands of tile, colored acoustical panels located on the wall in a geometric pattern, and an intricate floor pattern. Glazed overhead doors serve to close off the multipurpose meeting space from the circulation area.

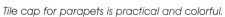
Tile cap for parapets is practical and colorful.

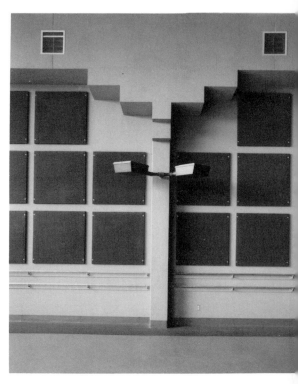

Sheetrock is shaped at piers to provide simple column capitals.

Warehouses converted to multiuse structures in Galveston historical area

Project: *Springer Building, Galveston, Texas*
Architects: *Taft Architects*
Date Completed: *1982*

Taft Architects were given the job of converting two Victorian warehouses into shops and apartments in the Strand Historical Area in Galveston. Their program called for four shops on the ground floor and eight apartments on the second and third floors. The entire project entailed 20,634 square feet (1917 square meters).

The buildings, designed by Nicholas Clayton, were stripped of their original facades in the 1930s. In 1978, the New York muralist, Richard Haas, designed and executed a trompe l'oeil painting on the street elevations of the two buildings.

DESIGN FEATURES

The high ceilings of the warehouse permitted mezzanines to be constructed as a second floor. The architects linked the two buildings at the second level with a two-story skylit atrium. In addition to providing vertical circulation and daylight to the apartments, this provided a common garden room that serves as a "front yard" for all the apartments.

In the apartment plans activity areas were organized around a central bathroom and kitchen core.

Special attention has been paid to the scale and color of the new architectural details to harmonize them with the scale and character of the original buildings.

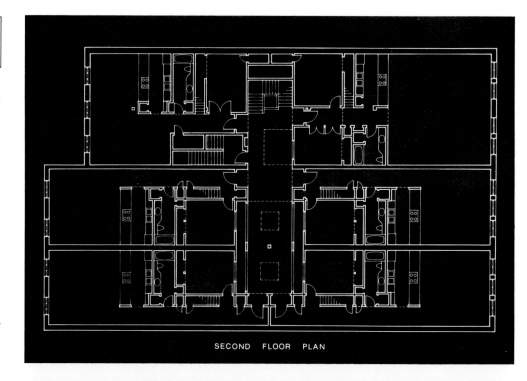

SECOND FLOOR PLAN

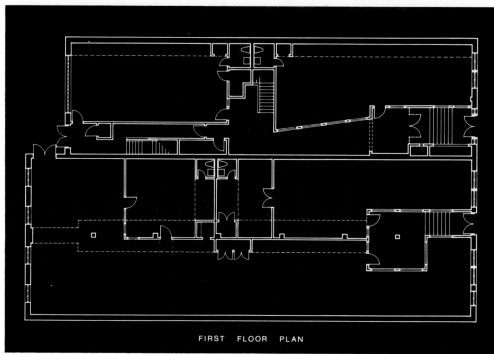

FIRST FLOOR PLAN

Top, above, right: Retail spaces are located on the ground floor of the Springer Building. A passage leads to a central hall that provides circulation to a skylit atrium above for access to the four apartments.

DESIGN/MANAGE TECHNIQUES

In addition to their organization of the interior, the architects designed a stencil pattern for the floors, which was executed by a friend of the owner. A single stencil, modest enough by itself, gained importance through repetition. The resultant pattern is used to create a processional way to a pair of apartments at the end of the corridor, handsomely identified by numbered medallions above the doors. Similar patterns at a smaller scale distinguish the entrance vestibules, flanking windows, and planted alcoves.

COST CONTROL

Costs were within original budget projections.

SCHEDULE

There were no scheduling problems.

Oversize numbers within medallions identify apartments, while the stenciled floor is complimented by painted moldings and window trim.

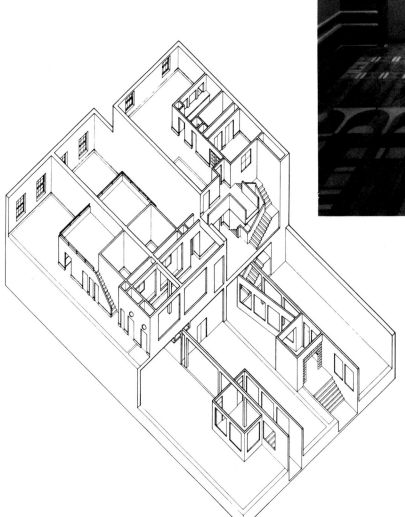

HELMUT C. SCHULITZ, ARCHITECT
Braunschweig, West Germany

Architect develops experimental housing system

Helmut C. Schulitz is a professor at the Technische Universitat Braunschweig and the Head of the Institute of Industrial Building in West Germany. His T.E.S.T. (Team for Experimental Systems-building Techniques) method grew out of a research and teaching position at the University of California at Los Angeles and has been developed over a 13-year period as a step toward establishing an industrialized building system.

Schulitz was convinced that certain developments in California showed great potential for the development of industrialized building techniques. He was specifically interested in projects developed by SCSD (School Construction Systems Development) and in the work of architects like Charles Eames and Raphael Soriano. Having worked in the field of building systems in Europe prior to his arrival in the United States, he focused on problems of multiuse building elements and the flexibility of buildings in general. With the T.E.S.T. program he set up a research direction whose goal was to develop building methods that allow the interchangeable use of off-the-shelf components.

The T.E.S.T. method consists of two parts:

1. The development of a catalog of compatible building elements.

2. A set of rules governing their combination.

The T.E.S.T. rules are an extension of the research done by the SAR group in Holland. These rules eliminate potential conflicts and guarantee predictable end, corner, and joint conditions. The T.E.S.T. method does not rely on any particular building material.

The criteria by which the components are selected for the T.E.S.T. catalog include maximum degree of factory preassembly, adaptability to existing on-site construction techniques, compatibility with other components, and the use of a standard dimensioning module. Catalog parts are based on a basic module of 4 inches (10 cm) , with the planning module of 1 foot (30 cm). The vertical module is 6 inches (15 cm).

The 4-inch module has been used in Europe and the United States for a number of years. It works with both metric and American dimensioning, so a smooth transition is ensured when the United States converts to the metric system.

Comparative accurate information from manufacturers about dimensions, product descriptions, cost, and delivery time is normally difficult to get. One purpose of the T.E.S.T. catalog is to provide such information and so save the architect many hours of thumbing through Sweets and other catalogs to locate compatible products. Building designs using the T.E.S.T. method do, by design, look unfinished and leave enough features to stimulate the imagination and input of those who use or occupy the space. Joining details

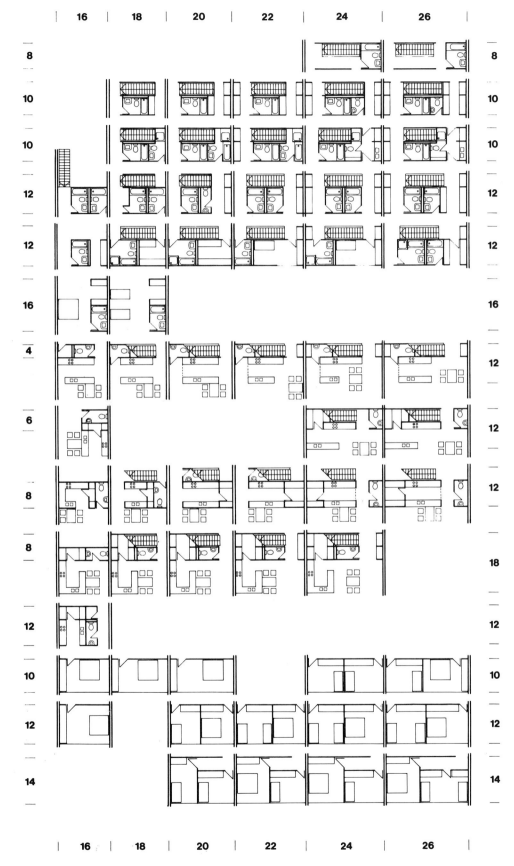

This chart shows plan variation for room types within the T.E.S.T. system. Numbers indicate the width of the units in feet.

are straightforward and rough, reflecting the inherent requirements of materials and assembly processes. Wood parts remain as rough as they are when they leave the factory. Welds are not ground, and nuts and bolts are not hidden. The system reflects the character of off-the-shelf components while still emphasizing systematic coordination. This system is based on the conviction that craftsmanship is an anachronism in building since the arrival of machine-made parts.

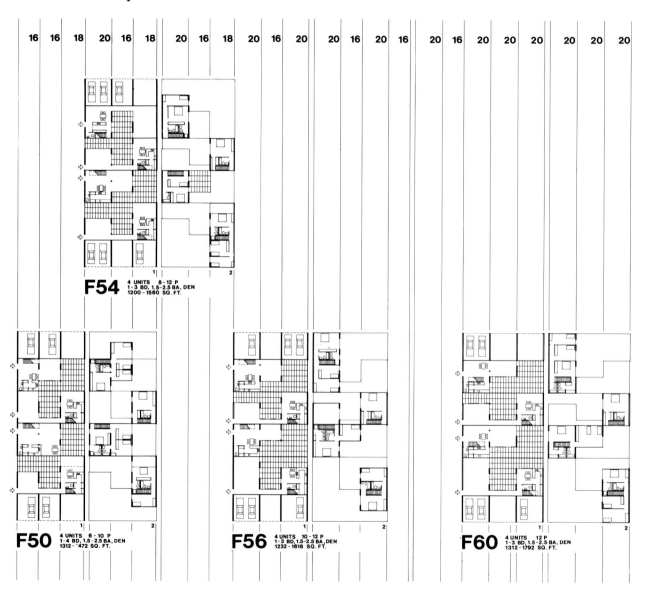

F54 4 UNITS   8 - 12 P
1 - 3 BD, 1.5 - 2.5 BA, DEN
1200 - 1560 SQ. FT.

F50 4 UNITS   6 - 10 P
1 - 4 BD, 1.5 - 2.5 BA, DEN
1312 - 1472 SQ. FT.

F56 4 UNITS   10 - 12 P
1 - 3 BD, 1.5 - 2.5 BA, DEN
1232 - 1616 SQ. FT.

F60 4 UNITS   12 P
1 - 3 BD, 1.5 - 2.5 BA, DEN
1312 - 1792 SQ. FT.

Subassemblies of rooms are shown in various combinations.

System of parts combines off-the-shelf components to cut costs

Project: *Hollywood houses, Los Angeles, California*
Architect: *Helmut C. Schulitz*
Date Completed: *1982*

These Hollywood houses were built to test the theories of the T.E.S.T. building method. The site is located in the foothills above Los Angeles and offers a view of the city and the Pacific Ocean. The houses are spacious, having 2000 and 2500 square feet (186 and 232 square meters) and only two bedrooms each. California energy legislation restricted a generous use of glass that would have been appropriate for the view. It was therefore necessary to plan the use of glass carefully, with windows oriented to the view, and concentrate them at the top of the buildings, since the view improves with height and only the view from the top floor cannot be blocked if the site below is redeveloped to the current zoning allowance.

DESIGN FEATURES

The houses reveal exposed industrial components such as bar joists, pipe railings, ductwork, electrical conduit, and steel industrial sash. These are picked out in bright primary colors. The overall appearance of the interiors is spacious and loftlike. The exterior is sheathed in metallic aluminum siding. A system of pipe trellises incorporates brightly colored awnings that control sunlight.

Above: Plans of the Hollywood houses are simple rectangles to accommodate the stock lengths of the structural members.

Right: Metal siding is combined with pipe supports for the awning system and stock metal windows on the exterior.

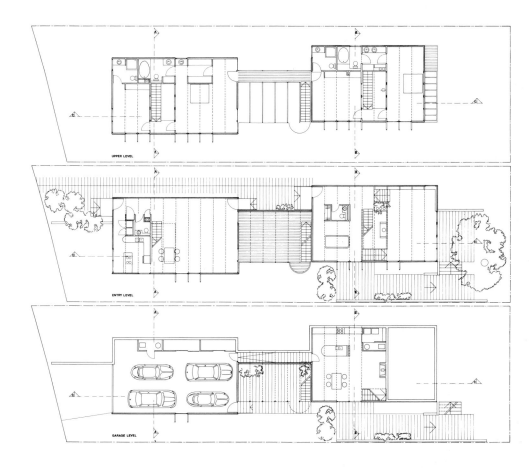

UPPER LEVEL

ENTRY LEVEL

GARAGE LEVEL

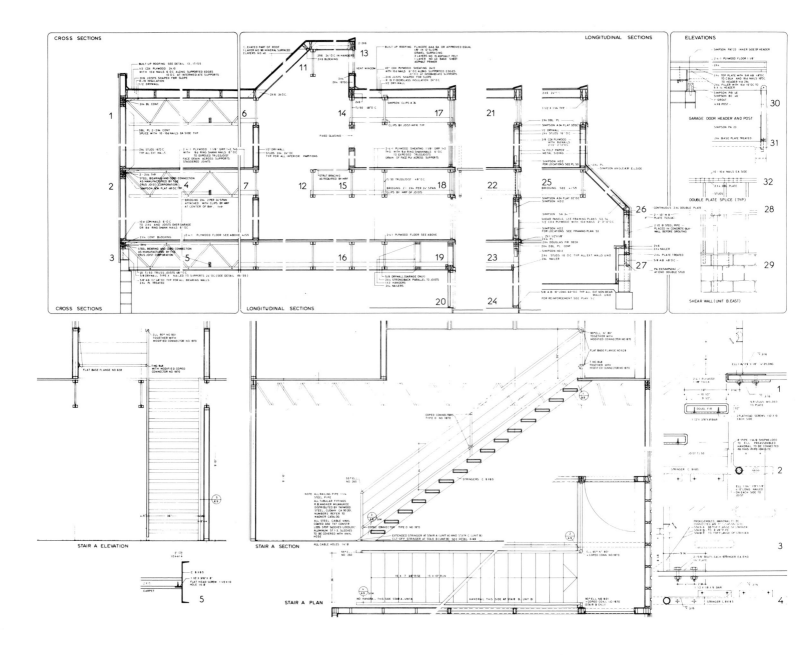

Above and opposite page right: Details call out stock components.

Opposite page left: The patterns of open web bar joists, pipe rails, and exposed electrical conduit are carefully controlled.

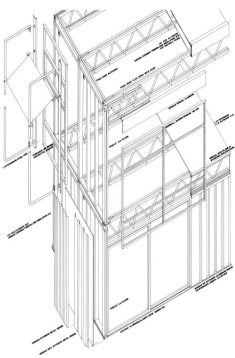

DESIGN/MANAGE TECHNIQUES

The houses are prototypes for the T.E.S.T. building method; however, a different set of structural elements other than the steel system that T.E.S.T. was designed for were used—standard lumber elements and components commonly used in California residential construction. In contrast with current California construction, the building demonstrates how material and labor can be saved through modular coordination. They are based on a 4-foot (1.2-meter) module and detailed so standard building elements sized 4′ × 8′ (1.2 × 2.4 m) can be used with little cutting or waste of material. Studs for all bearing walls are precut, and all studs for nonbearing walls have standard stud dimensions.

COST CONTROL

The houses were economically built, since the architect served as the general contractor.

SCHEDULE

The houses, built on schedule, were started in December 1981 and completed in October 1982. Completion would have been earlier, but it was delayed by a necessary business trip of Professor Schulitz in midsummer 1982.

A DESIGN GROUP, DAVID M. COOPER
Partners: Michael Folonis, Richard Clemensen, George Elian, Los Angeles, California

Architect/developer achieves design character with mundane items

To meet the low square-foot costs of their competitors, this architect/developer firm, A Design Group, headed by David M. Cooper, dramatizes the items that are frequently located without thought to design in this type of project. On the theory that these articles must be purchased anyway, things such as mailboxes, lighting fixtures, mechanical vents, chimneys, and water, power, telephone, and TV outlets are carefully located to provide design interest. Color is another important economical design aid. This detail emphasis is added to the staples of interesting design such as two-story spaces, unusual forms and surfaces, and location of windows and skylights for dramatic lighting.

A Design Group places one of their members in charge of each project, but frequent critique sessions are held with other team members.

First project as architect/designer/builder

Project: *831 Pacific Street, Santa Monica, California*
Architects/developers: *A Design Group*
Project Completion: *1981*

After completing several projects for developers, David Cooper of A Design Group decided to find out if he could avoid the design compromises often made in the name of economy by becoming a developer himself. In 1980 at the time of this project, a Santa Monica condominium boom was in progress, and the necessary financial backing came through at the same time as a narrow [53′ × 135′ (16 × 41 m)] lot close to the beach became available. To make a profitable project, the design task required six 1500-square-foot (139-square-meter) condominium units with two-car garages at a cost of $55 per square foot.

DESIGN FEATURES

The floor plans of the units are identical. Three living levels are on top of a subterranean garage. On the first level beside the entry there are two bedrooms and two baths. The second level contains living, dining, kitchen, bath, and exterior dining, above which is a mezzanine between two open-to-below volumes. From here, one can go up a stair to a roof sundeck. Bright yellow is used to accent floor lines on the exterior, and mechanical items such as vents and outlets are prominently displayed.

Left: Color accents the depth of the facade of the Santa Monica condominiums.

Below: The six units are identical on the exterior. Angled facades add individuality to each unit.

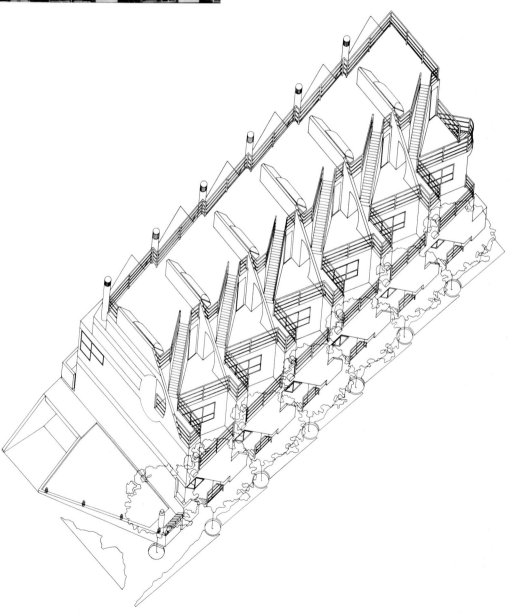

DESIGN/MANAGE TECHNIQUES

The design techniques used in the project have already been noted in the firm's general approach. To remain competitive, materials are restricted to builder's standards for this kind of structure in this area, basically stucco-clad woodframe with sheetrock interior wall finish and hardwood floors. One of the partners has a general contractor's license and the partners subcontracted all aspects of the work themselves. Due to their experience with this building type and subcontracting, this procedure worked. The main new aspect of the whole process was the financial one. Thanks to the fact that they capitalized almost a third of the project cost themselves, the banks were cooperative and cash flow was satisfactory.

COST CONTROL

Of the approximate $690,000 project cost, which included land and fees, the partners established a fund of $205,000 as their equity. After the units were sold, they prepaid the bank and distributed profits. Original estimates were good, thanks to experience on a previous similar project.

SCHEDULE

Subcontractors did their work within negotiated schedules, with the exception of the framing contractor who slowed the work down a month by his failure to show up on the job as promised. He was dismissed and a subsequent subcontractor completed the work. The overall job was completed in 10 months, only a month later than originally projected.

Bands of color mark the different floor levels.

Left: Interiors feature a two-story space.

Below: Use of pipe rails accents the openness of the spaces.

Bottom: Plans show skew elements and free-standing floors.

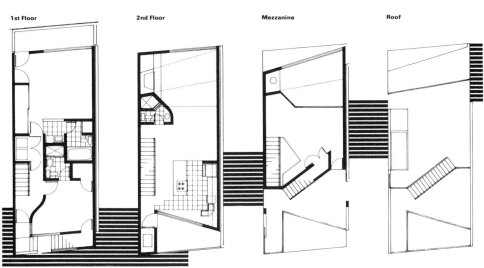

1st Floor **2nd Floor** **Mezzanine** **Roof**

JAMES STIRLING & MICHAEL WILFORD AND ASSOCIATES, CHARTERED ARCHITECTS

London, England, and Stuttgart, Germany

International firm combines bold forms with smaller-scale elements, color

This London-based firm has completed major noteworthy and award-winning institutional and educational buildings. At the concluding address to the 1980 Gold Metal presentation ceremony of the Royal Institute of British Architects, historian Mark Girouard suggested that the Stirling firm's design direction was difficult to classify. He chose three characteristics as major ones—shapeliness, delicacy, and gaiety. Girouard stated that all Stirling's buildings have "this terrifically elegant shape . . . are always delicate in scale, never overpowering . . . with a strong feeling for the scale of old cities . . . and a quality of gaiety, of entertaining one and giving one pleasure . . . a part of this is the element of color."

Stirling noted in his speech during the same ceremony that, for him, "the 'art' of architecture has always been *the priority*." He stated that the quality of the art of architecture, both at the time of building and in retrospect, is remembered as the significant element and that despite the ascendancy of sociological, functional, and real estate values in this century, the more ancient desire to see buildings as beautiful and appropriate to their context was returning. Stirling thinks that the visual language of early abstract modern architecture has become repetitive, simplistic, and confining and that we should now be able to include representational as well as abstract elements in our art.

English architects adapt to German construction techniques

Project: *Stuttgart Staatsgalerie, Stuttgart, West Germany*
Architects: *James Stirling & Michael Wilford and Associates*
Date Completed: *1984*

The City of Stuttgart selected James Stirling & Michael Wilford and Associates to do this project as the winners of a limited architectural competition. In addition to gallery space, the program called for a small theater, a recital hall, several experimental theaters, as well as a protected outdoor space for the exhibition of large sculpture. The building was to relate stylistically to the 19th-century classical gallery to which it is connected.

Site layout and town planning objectives were important since the planners wanted to move the public diagonally across the site, connecting a high landscaped terrace on one side of the building to a possible pedestrian bridge across another street. The creation of a new urban plaza was considered, continuing the street-oriented character in this area.

Within the building, programmers asked the architects to create a sequence of well-lit rooms, avoiding flexible space. They also asked for uninterrupted traffic flow between the old gallery and the new one, as well as for an encircled inner court to serve as a sculpture court and a circulation device between the two levels.

The Chamber Theater was to be sited near the Staatstheater across the street, and would ultimately connect with it via a pedestrian route. The Music School within the gallery would also connect with existing facilities and the gallery.

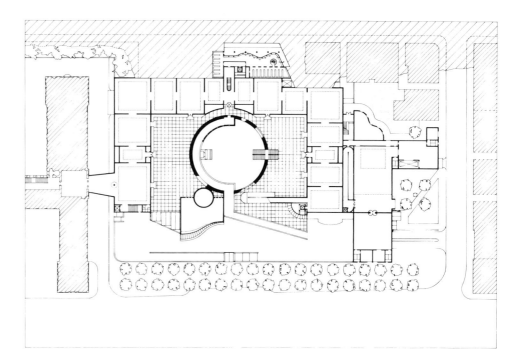

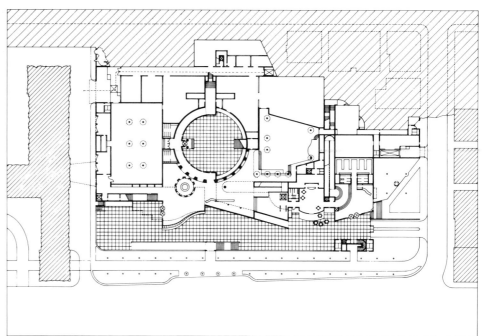

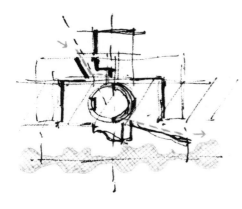

Left: The architects' original sketch shows the concept of the Stuttgart Staatsgalerie.

Top and above: Plans show the pedestrian route through the museum from the park at the top of the drawing to the street below.

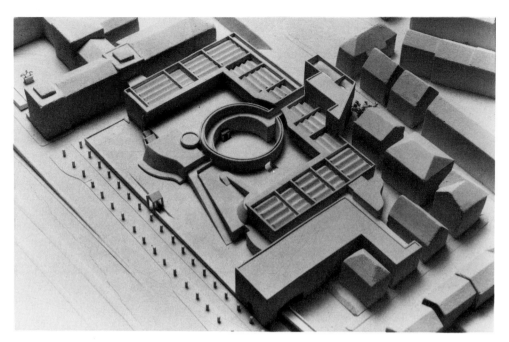

Block model illustrates the method of toplighting used for the galleries.

DESIGN/MANAGE TECHNIQUES

The architects quickly discovered that design and construction practices in West Germany were quite different from those of England. German architectural firms tend to specialize in either design or construction management, and larger firms often have partners specializing in both. Management people are designated as building leaders (*bauleiter*) and their role is similar to construction managers found on larger projects in the United States and the United Kingdom. However, the major difference in West Germany is the allegiance of these specialists to the architectural profession rather than the building industry.

As a result of this setup, general contractors are a rarity, and architects are responsible for the organization of the building process in addition to design and supervision.

Since this project was under the supervision of a public agency—the State of Baden Wurttemburg—a state building department wrote the specifications, authorized the tender lists, and administered the direction of construction. These factors, plus political pressure to begin site work as soon as possible, led the architects to establish a Stuttgart office under the direction of a local architect, Siggi Wernik.

Design direction was the responsibility of James Stirling, who visited the site every four weeks and approved all important decisions. The preparation of documents and the letting of contracts were done in Stuttgart. These numbered over 100 by the completion of the job.

Of great importance is the relationship of the masons to the work. In Stuttgart there are several family-run firms specializing in stonework. It is common for them to team up with one another on big jobs like this one, and for the lead firm of Albrecht Lauster, this job presented a major challenge. The architect requested bids on the basis of 1:100 elevations (⅛″ = 1′0″ approximately), leaving the successful bidder responsible for the preparation and submission of detail drawings.

COST CONTROL

The budget was continuously updated as subcontracts were let.

DESIGN FEATURES

The building makes stylistic overtures to the adjacent 19th-century gallery building and opera house across the street, but has a number of unusual 20th-century features that make it difficult to assign it to any of the current stylistic directions prevalent in the world. The street facades are mostly clad in stone, interrupted by unusual features such as a warped glazed wall that is the exterior of the entrance hall and a steel-and-glass canopy overlapping a shallow arched opening.

Within, the center of the building is occupied by a circular sculpture court open to the sky. The walls of this are pierced by big unornamented windows; a wide staircase emerges through one of them. A semicircular ramp occupies the other side of the drum, winding its way up to the second floor of the building. The galleries, which form the bulk of the building, are toplit and have a covered cornice on the exterior, capping the stone walls. The exterior is clad in 1½-inch thick (38-mm) slabs of travertine marble and local sandstone, laid up in alternate courses. The attachment of these to the concrete structure is unusual, since they are positioned 3 inches (76 mm) out from the inner wall by stainless steel anchors, with the joints open and the void filled with a glass fiber insulating quilt. This important detail required careful coordination with the subcontractors.

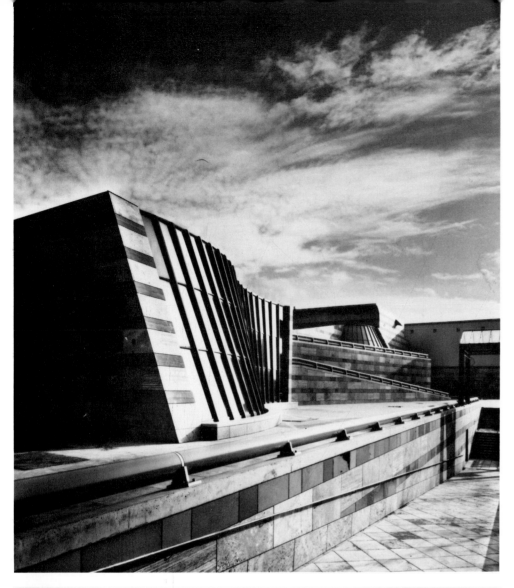

Left: The entrance area features a combination of ramps and a skew window.

Above: This closeup view of the entrance area shows the open joints of the stone attachment system.

Below: Stonework is combined with stucco and metal awning tack-ons.

SCHEDULE

Due to pressures to get the work done quickly, the coordination of architectural, structural, mechanical, and acoustical services in London and Stuttgart went on continuously through the job once the first contract was let in June 1979. This method of working is considered a fast-track job, unusual in the United States and the United Kingdom, but normal in West Germany.

BUMPZOID

Partners: Ben Benedict, Carl Pucci
New York, New York

Architects' background as builders helps in their practice

When Ben Benedict and Carl Pucci were students in New Haven, Connecticut, they ran separate light contracting operations during their holidays and summers. At that time, projects were designed and built by them, often with minimal or no drawings. Details were worked out on-site and their daily involvement during the construction phase enabled them to work out innovative solutions to the projects. Their construction abilities also helped get them architectural jobs, since owners generally think that a design/build operation will control costs more closely than a separate design firm that sends out for competitive bids.

After graduation Benedict and Pucci formed BumpZoid and relocated to New York. The firm is moving away from their earlier philosophy and stressing their design abilities, which they have found more to their liking than coordinating subcontractors. Clients are advised that jobs will be bid conventionally. However, the architects feel that their background in contracting enables them to produce construction documents that will meet their client's budgets.

BumpZoid distributes an extensive questionnaire to each client at the beginning of the job. The architects insist that the clients complete this form, from which they attempt to determine traffic and other patterns of living or working and also to learn about the dimensional and psychological preferences of the building's occupants.

"Ordinary" Cape Cod house is transformed

Project: *Niejelow/Rodin rebuilding, Stratford, Connecticut*
Architects: *BumpZoid*
Date Completed: *1980*

When the owners of this suburban house were dissatisfied with its conventional appearance and layout, but wanted to retain it for its waterview, they appealed to BumpZoid for a programmatic and visual change of pace. The owners wanted the redo to be quite contemporary and to incorporate some of their enthusiasm for visual imagery.

Left: The Niejelow/Rodin house looked like this before renovation.

Below: After renovation, the house became more striking visually, which was one of the client's program demands.

DESIGN FEATURES

The architects held the front building line, but stripped off two bay windows and raised the roof and front wall. All windows that existed previously were eliminated, and a series of awning windows combined with smaller fixed windows were substituted. The architects believed that the location of this house by the sea demanded a powerful image to coexist with the dominant seascape. To this end, they designed a zigzag roof line, a grouped window pattern, and whimsical touches such as a wavy pipe rail on top of the projecting front entry. Textural interest was added by varying the spacing of shingles from top to bottom.

DESIGN/MANAGE TECHNIQUES

Emphasizing an ability to fulfill client's needs by careful design, the architects distributed a four-page form listing 68 questions for the clients to answer. The questionnaire is prefaced by the following:

"This is a group of questions to get you to think about how you would like your life and your living space to interact. Ideals and aspirations, no matter how impractical or ridiculous, are as important to note down as very practical and mundane things. Try to keep in mind how things look, sound, smell, and feel. Think about the flow of food, materials, people, and stuff that moves through your environment. And try to indicate the parts of the routine that get you down the most or, conversely, that you enjoy the most. (Remember that the seasons may have a large effect on things.)

"We're aiming to get a detailed, abstract picture of what you do in order to choose the sort of environment in which it is best to do it. As a rule, prejudgments about sizes and other specifics aren't very helpful unless they have particular bearing on the situation (i.e., the study needs to accommodate a canvas 8′ × 10′ [2.4 × 3 m]). By picturing exactly what you want, you run the risk of overlooking the best alternative. Anyway, you might as well let the architects work for their fee."

Some of the clients' questions and answers were as follows:

Q.: Is there a particular height off the floor that the bed must be to make you feel comfortable?
A.: 26 inches [66 cm] with 28-inch (71-cm) night table.

Q.: Do you like to use the bathroom in a leisurely or hurried fashion?
A.: Leisurely.

Q.: What times of day, for what purpose, and to what extent would you like to use your kitchen?
A.: To eat meals in, be the central focus of our day-to-day activities. We love to cook.

Q.: Do you like to be be able to look out the window while you're working in the kitchen?
A.: Yes, but could look into a greenhouse.

Q.: What sort of feeling should the dining place have?
A.: Airy, spacious, warm.

Q.: Do you feel a need for a guest (i.e., formal) dining area separate from a family (i.e., informal) dining area?
A.: Yes.

Q.: Do you spend a lot or a little time at the dinner table?
A.: We'll eat in the kitchen.

Q.: Are there certain activities that would be restricted from taking place in the living area?
A.: Eating meals.

Q.: What sort of artificial lighting would be compatible with your image of the living space?
A.: Track.

Q.: List all the rooms or activity areas that are necessary, with a clarifying note on any that haven't been covered.
A.: Study: desk facing water, good lighting, good storage; guest bedroom: private; entry foyer: must be an interesting

statement and able to hold people comfortably; consideration that the doorway from the garage into kitchen may be widely used and entry should be neat.

Q.: What is your attitude toward dirt . . . where you do and don't mind it, and how often you clean it up?
A.: O.K. outside and in greenhouse. Will hate it being tracked on kitchen floor; we hate cleaning!

Q.: What sort of textures do you like?
A.: Light wood grains, nubby fabrics, thickness, stainless steel, plastic.

Q.: Do you like vertical or horizontal spaces or both?
A.: Both.

Q.: List your favorite buildings and what makes them special.
A.: Yale hockey rink—open feeling, novelty. Some of Charlie Gwathmey's early houses and his latest one in the Hamptons. World Trade Center because it has so much glass and demands attention. Beineke Rare Book Library—interplay of light and textures. We like smooth, contoured angles and interesting juxtapositions.

The architects believe that the clients' answers were important in fulfilling their needs. However, the architects admit that the answer concerning favorite buildings and what makes them special had little tangible effect on the ultimate design.

COST CONTROL

Costs were kept close to the budget, thanks to the clients' buying some items such as windows separately. Although there was a general contractor throughout the job, other economies were made, such as subcontracting separately for the plumbing work.

SCHEDULE

The bulk of the work took place during a three-month period. Finishing touches went on for another year.

Handrail curves are carried throughout the house.

Interiors were opened up and details devised to convey the new image of the house.

KOJI YAGI
Tokyo, Japan

Professor designs houses as adjunct to teaching

Dr. Koji Yagi has had worldwide experience in the research and academic areas of the architectural profession, and he has studied and taught in the United States, the Middle East, China, and Southeast Asia, in addition to his native Japan. From these diverse influences, he brings a fresh outlook to his work as practicing architect.

Dr. Yagi has worked with a diversity of structural and cladding materials, frequently combining them in original ways. He is interested in the thermal performance of buildings and has devised envelopes that work efficiently in the Japanese climate.

Dr. Yagi has also tailored his efforts to varying client demands. He notes that architects in Japan do not always provide complete professional services. Since there is a strong vernacular tradition in housing, it is possible for an architect to do simple plans, elevations, and sections and turn these over to a carpentry company with confidence that the house will be well executed technically and esthetically. Strong working relationships exist between architects and builders, and they collaborate with an exchange of drawings, thereby expanding one another's skills. Since litigation is rare in Japan, there is little danger of this kind of collaboration resulting in monetary claims if something goes wrong in the building process.

There are also practicing architectural groups within construction companies and in department stores, which offer prefabricated dwellings to their customers, tailoring them as required.

Graphic designer's house is a collaborative effort

Project: *Shigeo Fukuda house, Tokyo, Japan*
Architect: *Dr. Koji Yagi*
Date Completed: *1983*

The client for this house—one of Tokyo's leading graphic designers—collaborated on all aspects of its design with the architect. Three areas were required: a studio for the designer, another for his daughter who is an art student, and living areas (living room, kitchen, wife's room, bath, and utility room). Each of the three areas contains one bedroom for the respective member of the family. All are connected by a two-story entrance hall that also serves as a gallery and library. The entire area was 3200 square feet (297 square meters).

DESIGN FEATURES

To amuse himself and his friends, the client fancied an illusory entrance. After some experimentation, the architect and client settled on a trapezoidal opening in an equally trapezoidal "billboard" that would serve as the entrance facade. Straight ahead within this is a trompe l'oeil corridor with walls, ceiling, and floor that all slope toward a half-size door set at eye level. The true entrance, out of sight, is down a trapezoidal corridor at right angles to the fake entrance immediately inside the entrance billboard.

Beyond this entrance, the main house is a simple rectangle below a gable roof. This contains a large studio—the entire second floor is used by the graphic artist—below which is his daughter's studio and the family living quarters on the ground floor. A small attic is positioned above the large second floor studio.

A complex arrangement of spaces exists between the first and second floor studios. The second floor studio contains a stepped display area for art as well as a portion of the owner's large collection of "fake food" (one of the important collections of this type). The bottom of the stepped area forms a lively stepped ceiling in the daughter's studio below.

The skew door and trompe l'oeil false door were requested by the owner of this house in Tokyo.

Thermal performance was an important consideration in this building. There is no air conditioning, so cross ventilation in all rooms is provided. Additionally, the large studio on the second floor is divided into two parts. The larger high-ceilinged part is unheated and can be closed off in winter from the smaller south-facing heated part by a row of sliding doors.

DESIGN/MANAGE TECHNIQUES

The client is a graphic designer for Matsuya department store, which is one of Tokyo's leading retailers. Since they have an architectural/construction department that customizes a line of prefabricated building components, the client asked the architect if he would be willing to work in collaboration with the Matusya people to produce the necessary design drawings. Architect and designer worked out the basic design and submitted the preliminary designs to Matsuya's architectural-contracting office, which suggested modifications. These were incorporated and returned to Matsuya for final working drawings. Subcontractors were then selected by Matsuya. They prepared shop drawings for the architect's approval, who then passed them down the approval chain for final execution. The architect maintained liaison with the client at all critical approval stages.

COST CONTROL

Initial cost estimates were 20 percent above the budget. Negotiations and modifications succeeded in bringing the price down to budget.

SCHEDULE

Design work took six months. Construction took five months.

Left: The side of the house is simply detailed in steel.

Below: This axonometric drawing shows the relationship of the house to its front facade.

Bottom: Elevation shows skew front.

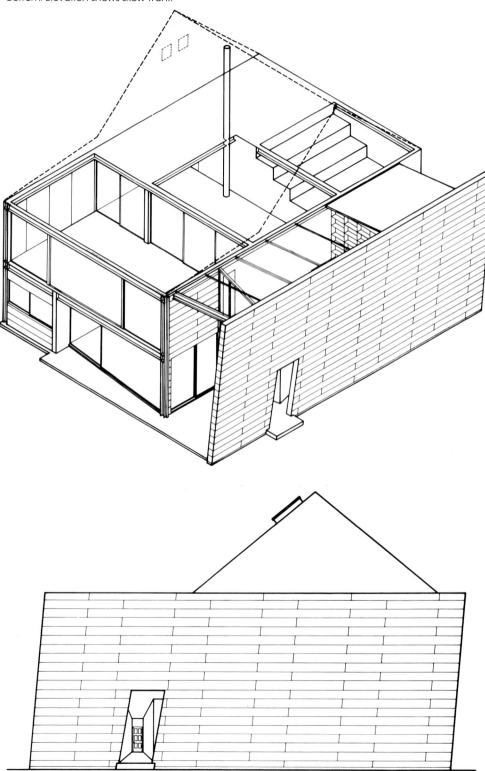

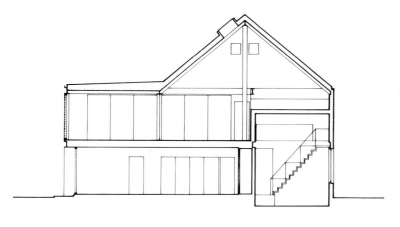

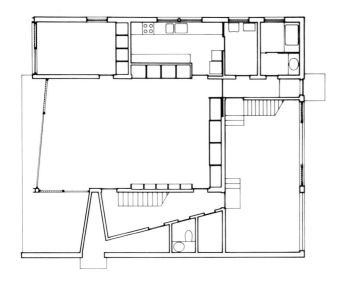

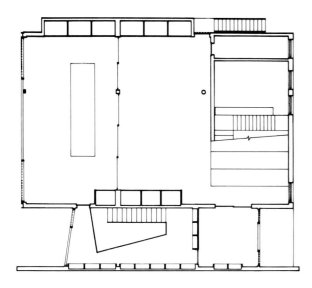

Far left top: The rectangular main body of the house is contained below a pitched roof, while the entrance area is under a flat roof.

Far left middle and bottom: Most of the house is contained in a rectangular plan. The entrance area and gallery are arranged behind the billboard entrance facade.

Left: The second floor of the entrance area is covered with a skylight. It contains the owner's library.

Below: Steel grids in the studio are painted in bright primary colors. The stepped area with a display of art objects is over the other studio.

ARNOLD SYROP ASSOCIATES, ARCHITECTS
New York, New York

Architect stresses client relationships, tailored construction procedures

Some of Arnold Syrop's work is done with a specific client who generates enough work to employ a contractor full time. This ongoing and close relationship between contractor and owner requires the architect to tailor his design efforts to the owner's particular method of working. This encourages mutual feedback and a final design that reflects the ideas of both parties.

Other work done by this office includes houses, renovations, and professional and corporate offices. Design and construction approaches are adapted to the individual job, with some work subcontracted separately to save time or money for the owner.

Found objects are featured in midtown restaurant

Project: *Manhattan Ocean Club, New York, New York*
Architect: *Arnold Syrop Associates, Architects*
Date Completed: *1984*

The Manhattan Ocean Club is the third of a trio of restaurants conceived by the owner with Arnold Syrop the same architect. Their previous experience together enabled them to work efficiently, using the same basic approach employed on the other two establishments. The program called for an elegant atmosphere featuring fresh seafood, good lighting, distinctive decor, and attractive furnishings. An overall sense of spacious luxuriousness was the predominant feeling requested by the owner.

DESIGN FEATURES

Since the Manhattan Ocean Club is located in space vacated by another restaurant, extensive structural alterations were not required. However, the menu and decor were to have an entirely different character, and these became the areas of concentration for the owner and architect.

Both the restauranteur and the architect are admirers of art objects and architectural fragments in particular, which became the highlight of the design. Of interest in themselves, these objects are enhanced by their juxtaposition with other architectural detailing.

Above: Some spaces, such as this, were part of the previous restaurant. The architect gave them new identity in the Manhattan Ocean Club through decorative accents, lighting, and surface treatment.

The plans provide an entrance bar area that flows through a narrow neck to the main dining area.

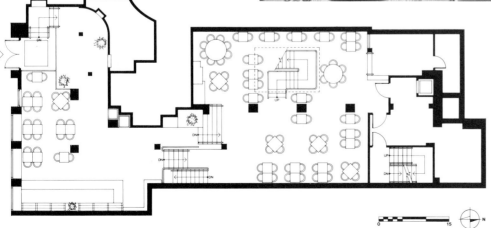

DESIGN/MANAGE TECHNIQUES

An outline of the design and construction sequence follows:

Week 1. The owner selected the site and signed his leasing deal after the architect reviewed the site and provided a rough renovation budget.

Week 3. The architect reviewed a general space allocation concept with the owner.

Week 4. a. The architect prepared a preliminary construction budget including decor items and kitchen equipment.

b. The owner's contractor started demolition under a fixed-fee arrangement with a bonus for early completion.

c. The architect started preliminary design development at the same time and finalized bathroom and office areas using 8½″ × 11″ (22 × 28 cm) sketches.

Week 5. a. The owner and architect began a search for found objects.

b. The architect determined basic functional relationships, including the location of bars, the stairway, coatcheck, maitre d' service areas, and waiters stations.

c. A structural engineer was brought in to consult on the structural consequences of new floor openings.

Week 6. a. The owner consulted his staff to finalize kitchen and kitchen service relationships and required equipment areas. Kitchen equipment built by the previous owner was retained and modified.

b. The contractor started construction on bathrooms and office areas.

c. The architect developed the major design concept and key details. In this case, the typical column detail and niche details were important. The owner and architect are both interested in sculpture and used three-dimensional art, sculpture niches, and found architectural objects as a theme in their previous restaurants.

Week 7. The contractor laid out the partitions with his crew and built the columns to be decorated by the found artifacts. Existing stairways were demolished where they were no longer required.

Week 8. A lighting consultant was brought in to develop lighting concepts and the electrical plan.

Week 11. a. The architect started stair detail development using 8½″ × 11″ sketches in consultation with the structural engineer, who designed the new framing.

b. The architect designed the bars.

c. The contractor updated the budget, based on the new drawings.

Week 13. a. The contractor let a subcontract for the sheetrock ceiling and started construction. Lighting fixtures were ordered.

b. Kitchen equipment requirements were decided and a subcontract let.

Week 15. a. Architectural objects were prepared, cleaned, and delivered by the supplier, Urban Archaeology.

b. The owner and architect finalized details and finishes for table bases, table tops, and seating and dishware. Orders were placed.

c. Final materials and color selections were made.

Week 16. The architect approved a custom handrail detail for all railings after making a full-scale mockup. The railings and wood fluted columns were ordered.

Week 17. The owner started to collect Picasso ceramics for display niches.

Week 20. The contractor started wood flooring installation and construction of the bars on site.

Week 22. a. Sheetrock work was completed.

b. The contractor installed the architectural artifacts.

Week 23. Terrazzo floors and kitchen equipment were installed.

Week 24. a. Lacquer light boxes and display niches were installed.

b. Glazing, mirrors, and marble tile were installed.

Week 26. a. Painting and stair installation were completed. Wood rails were installed and stained.

b. The restaurant was opened on the lower floor while punch-list items were worked on and construction was completed on the upper floor.

COST CONTROL

There was an approximate budget set at the beginning of the job, which was continually adjusted as the design evolved.

SCHEDULE

The system of doing design work while construction proceeded resulted in completion earlier than would have been possible with conventional approaches.

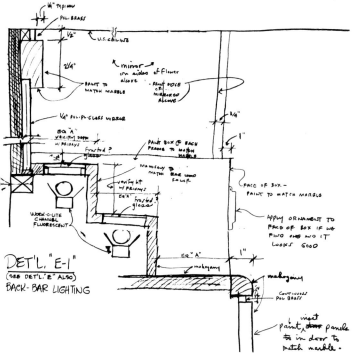

DET'L. "E-1"
(SEE DET'L. "E" ALSO)
BACK-BAR LIGHTING

Above: Lighting was an important factor in the bar design. A lighting designer was employed on a consulting basis.

Left: This sketch explained the design of the bar to the builder.

Below: This enclosure for the owner's collection of Picasso plates was detailed freehand in the field (see right), once existing conditions were determined.

Right: Freehand sketches supplemented hard-line drawings to solve specific problems.

Bottom: Detail drawings such as this were prepared to instruct the contractor.

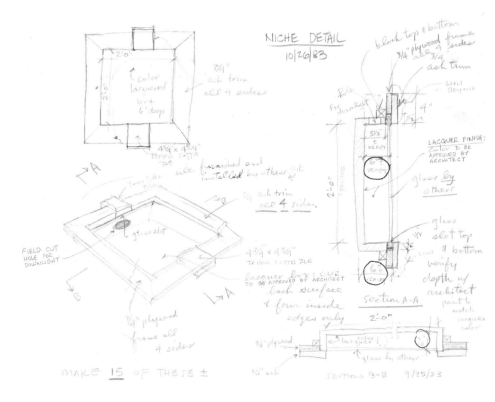

NICHE DETAIL
10/26/83

MAKE 15 OF THESE ±

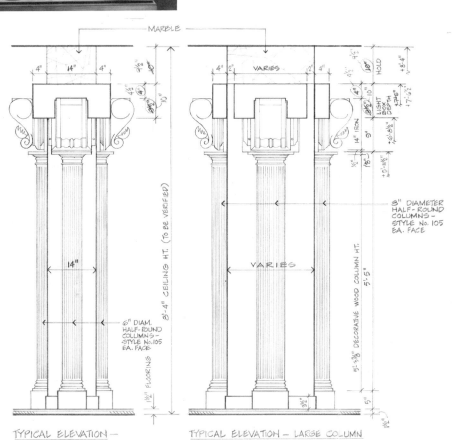

TYPICAL ELEVATION –
SMALL COLUMN

TYPICAL ELEVATION – LARGE COLUMN

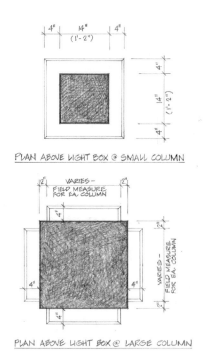

PLAN ABOVE LIGHT BOX @ SMALL COLUMN

PLAN ABOVE LIGHT BOX @ LARGE COLUMN

A pipe rail was transformed into something elegant through the use of fluted wood add-ons.

WILLIAM T. CANNADY & ASSOCIATES, INC., ARCHITECTS
Houston, Texas

Development projects are adjunct to architectural practice

The firm of William T. Cannady & Associates, Inc., Architects, is noted for its design quality. The firm specializes in the rehabilitation of existing buildings, additions, and interior design. Development work undertaken by William Cannady does not represent more than 5 percent of the project workload in the office at any given time. Although development work is financially more rewarding, Cannady wants to remain an actively practicing architect. He notes that the architectural firm's experience in renovation work enables him to control costs and schedules in his development work, as well as spot a good opportunity when he sees one.

Renovation provides good development opportunity

Project: *Village Square, Houston, Texas*
Architect: *William T. Cannady & Associates, Inc., Architects*
Date Completed: *1984*

Located in Houston's earliest suburban shopping center called The Village, this project was to revitalize a group of 30-year-old, mostly vacant buildings. The buildings contained 17,000 square feet (1579 square meters) of retail and 16,000 square feet (1486 square meters) of office space. They were in good structural shape but ugly, with discordant proportions, colors, textures, and signs.

Interiors were poorly lit by high strip windows only 1 foot (31 cm) tall that did not permit occupants to look out. Previous interior renovations had produced a maze of spaces that were not commercially attractive.

DESIGN FEATURES

Various properties were combined under a single ownership, and the rear parking was reorganized to allow for additional parking and loop circulation around the complex. Landscaping was added with emphasis on street trees. The exterior elevations were significantly altered by enlarging the upper windows, stuccoing over the tile and stone panels, and adding pediments over the entries. The composition was unified by the use of horizontal black awnings over the sidewalks that contrasted with two light yellow pedimented entry pavilions. Brick was painted a terra-cotta color. Perimeter lighting located at the coping accents the facades at night.

The interior was completely gutted. Public areas were reorganized to emphasize circulation areas. New tenant lease space was designed to emphasize high ceilings, with the steel and concrete structure expressed. Interior colors are variations of gray with muted red and blue accents.

A handsome rendering like this is useful in presenting a concept to potential lessors.

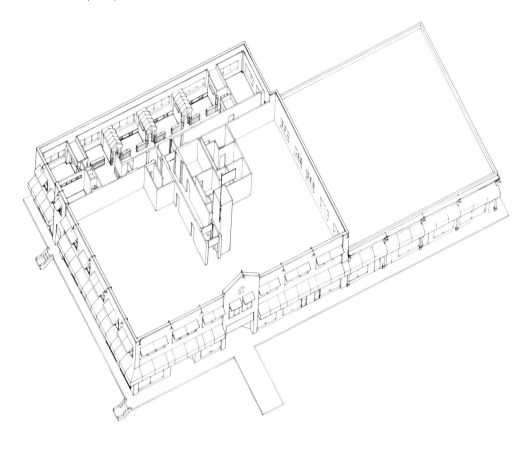

This axonometric drawing of the Village Square shows the relationship of the entrance areas to the rentable open spaces.

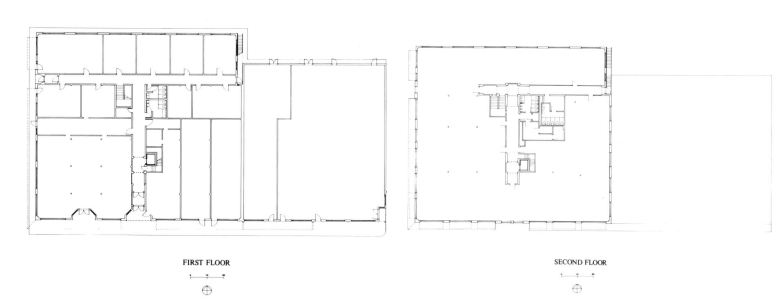

FIRST FLOOR

SECOND FLOOR

DESIGN/MANAGE TECHNIQUES

The architect, who has done other development projects over the last decade, states the importance of borrowing sufficient money to cover all project costs. He in fact paid a fee to his architectural firm from the amount borrowed from the bank to cover the entire development. He thinks it is a mistake to finance development projects with income derived from an architectural firm, since smaller architectural firms do not have sufficient cash flow to permit this. Development costs for this project totaled approximately $2.5 million; of this roughly 65 percent represented the cost of the property. Of the remaining 35 percent, rehabilitation costs were 17 percent, fees 7 percent, and financing 8 percent, and 3 percent went toward an operating account that covered negative cash flow while the building was being rented. This last item, sometimes overlooked, may cause the developer severe financial problems if it has not been planned for. A small architectural office would certainly be unable to carry the burden out of operating income.

COST CONTROL

Due to previous development experience and a strong background doing this kind of work for others in the architectural office, the architect was able to stay within original cost projections.

SCHEDULE

The original construction schedule was met. The building is renting quickly in an otherwise oversaturated Houston market, probably due to its attractiveness and appeal to those firms and businesses requiring small space.

Opposite page top: Project view shows close adherence to the original concept.

Opposite page bottom left and right: Plans show creation of large open areas for leasing purposes.

Below: Attractive corridors were an important selling feature.

ROLAND SIMOUNET
Paris, France

Completed buildings by Paris-based architect reflect follow through on early ideas

Roland Simounet stresses the use of a single material in his buildings, generally masonry units or concrete, and organizes it in crisp geometric forms. His office is unusual for a Parisian-based firm, since it is small and all aspects of the work are directly supervised by Simounet. The firm's work is varied and current jobs include houses, housing, and museums.

The design direction of the office emphasizes different kinds of wall building that are determined by the resolution of a particular construction problem. An attempt is made to build walls in accordance with the nature of their materials as Simounet visualizes it. For instance, in a joint between a concrete wall superimposed on a brick wall, great emphasis is placed on a clean joint without reveal or dripping of the concrete onto the brick. Subterfuge in the use of materials is not allowed even in the formwork for the concrete. Instead, the design is altered to fit the nature of the building process.

Another of Simounet's interests is the conduction of rainwater. The architect's solution is usually a series of scuppers that conduct the water on the roof to splash blocks on the ground below, rather than through internal drains. He likes these because rain transforms the scuppers into little waterfalls that continue to flow even after the rain has ceased. Gutters and spillways are arranged so they can be seen by the users of the building. Scuppers are positioned to avoid staining the wall below, as Simounet has observed many examples of Renaissance architecture disfigured by such staining.

Simounet's work also shows a preoccupation with the classic emphasis on wall openings by surrounding them with piers and lintels resting on these piers. Joints between the two are articulated to give the impression of lightness. This can often give the facade a fragmented picturesque look despite the simplicity of the elements. All these elements give the building a strong silhouette against the sky.

Simounet uses simple line drawings to study his work and explain ideas to the client. Models are not in evidence in the office, and clients are discouraged from altering the designs after a design direction has been set.

House built with indigenous techniques compares favorably with prefabricated structures

Project: *Vacation house, Corsica, France*
Architects: *Roland Simounet*
Date Completed: *1969*

While visiting friends, the architect felt challenged when shown a catalog of prefabricated houses that they were considering for a vacation house on Corsica. The architect knew the site, a 500-square-foot (46-square-meter) dune at the edge of the Tyrrhenian Sea, and suggested that he study an alternate building type, one more appropriate to the area that used indigenous construction techniques.

The program was simple: a major sleeping/living room, a smaller children's room, a kitchen, and a shower/toilet facility. But the sandy location, the glare of the sun, and the lack of water or electricity all had to be taken into account. There were to be two entrances: one for "dry feet" and one for "wet feet," which was near a rinse-off shower. A flagstone terrace extending the house was to be equipped with an outdoor grill.

The piers surrounding the window openings of this vacation house on Corsica not only give a classic look but provide shading and shelter from sun and sand.

The location of the house on the sandy beach is an important reason for raising the terraces and floor levels.

Left: Detail closeup reveals jointing pattern of the locally manufactured concrete block.

Below: Pavilions provide shade and shelter for outdoor cooking. Note the careful joining of concrete and roof slab with the block-supporting piers.

DESIGN FEATURES

A local stone building technique was used to construct the walls and local lava slabs were used for the terrace. The amount of ventilation is adjustable via deflectors. Pavements can be hosed down, with excess water carried off by shallow gutters. Deep overhangs provide protection from the sun for walls and openings. Protection from insects is provided by shutters and mosquito netting on the adjustable deflectors, while protection from the sand is provided by raised thresholds at the doors. Pine needles, which accumulate in profusion, can be flushed off the terraces into the gutters by a system using trapped rainwater.

DESIGN/MANAGE TECHNIQUES

The work was accomplished with simple drawings that called for structural members and repetitive indigenous masonry techniques. Much of the detailing was done on-site by workers experienced enough in this kind of construction to use skill in putting materials together. The key strategy of the architect was to enlist the cooperation of the builders by doing things their way.

COST CONTROL

The cost of the structure without equipment was less than the prefabricated building originally considered by the owner.

SCHEDULE

Construction took five months and was completed in time for the summer vacation period for which it was designed.

Provence house is built in accordance with early conceptual sketches

Project: *House, Provence, France*
Architect: *Roland Simounet*
Date Completed: *1980*

Views of the Mediterranean and the chalky mountains of Provence were important site conditions in the planning of this house. Programmatically, the client requested wide separation of guest, children's, and master bedrooms and a corresponding separation of functions in the spacious principal room.

The clients, who were originally from Morocco, referred to the spatial idea of a casbah, intending a series of diverse spaces housing different functions. The whole house occupies 6000 square feet (557 square meters).

DESIGN FEATURES

Given the owners' thoughts on space distribution and organization, Roland Simounet quotes Le Corbusier when speaking of the "promenade architecture" qualities of his design. He is referring to the connections of the many cubical elements by stairs and ramps. These occur both inside and out and serve to set the house in the sloping landscape.

The forms are reinforced by the material called "breeze-block." It is a crudely made rough cement block, which was chosen for its decorative aspect. The jointing pattern is raised, accenting the modularity of the material in oblique light.

Within, decor and built-in furniture of a massive sort reflect the owner's desire for Moroccan forms. These are softened by many richly patterned cushions.

Cubic masses are combined with piers around openings in this house in Provence.

The stepped patio was built according to the original sketches.

Masonry wings serve as retaining walls to fit the house into the landscape.

DESIGN/MANAGE TECHNIQUES

After noting the owners' program and esthetic preferences, the architect made a series of conceptual sketches early in his design studies. He is proud of the fact that the final result closely duplicates these and points out his devotion to original ideas as responsible for the excellent design reputation of his firm. When asked whether the client questioned any of his recommendations, he pointed out that his study of their original requirements precluded that possibility.

COST CONTROL

Costs were within original projections, thanks to the use of breeze-block, which is noted for its cheapness. Although this material is generally not intended to be exposed, the architect used it carefully in this house with good results.

SCHEDULE

The primary material had been extensively used locally, and the work proceeded without schedule holdups.

Jointing of breeze block provides textural interest on broad expanses of flat wall.

LIST OF DESIGNERS

INDEX OF PHOTOGRAPHERS

Edited by Stephen A. Kliment and Susan Davis
Designed by Jay Anning
Graphic production by Hector Campbell
Set in 10 point Century Old Style